NORTHROP FRYE
AND THE POETICS OF PROCESS
Caterina Nella Cotrupi

Caterina Nella Cotrupi's *Northrop Frye and the Poetics of Process* sheds a new conceptual light on Frye, successfully bringing him back into the central ring of contemporary critical thought. Challenging the often dismissive view of Frye's work as closed and outdated, Dr Cotrupi explores the implications of his proposition that the history of criticism may be seen as having two main approaches – literature as 'product' and literature as 'process.' In focusing on Frye's exploration of the process tradition Cotrupi sheds light on the agenda that Frye established for himself when he noted at the end of *Anatomy of Criticism* that the reconciliatory task of criticism was to 'reforge the broken link between creation and knowledge, art and science, myth and concept.'

Dr Cotrupi recontextualizes Frye's thought and shows us how Frye continues to be not only relevant but central to a number of the key concerns in the contemporary critical scene. Re-examining Frye's place in the history of critical thought, Dr Cotrupi builds upon Frye's original vision of the 'process' tradition and suggests further directions this exploration may take. Among the current areas of critical engagement which Cotrupi examines are relativism, possible world theory, and postmodernism – making this work of interest not only to Frye scholars, but also to those interested in the debates currently rocking the world of criticism, literature, and culture.

(Frye Studies)

CATERINA NELLA COTRUPI is a lawyer and educator in Toronto.

NORTHROP FRYE
AND THE
POETICS OF PROCESS

Caterina Nella Cotrupi

UNIVERSITY OF TORONTO PRESS
Toronto Buffalo London

© University of Toronto Press Incorporated 2000
Toronto Buffalo London
Printed in Canada

ISBN 0-8020-4316-X (cloth)
ISBN 0-8020-8141-X (paper)

Printed on acid-free paper

Frye Studies

Canadian Cataloguing in Publication Data

Cotrupi, Caterina Nella, 1953–
  Northrop Frye and the poetics of process

  Includes bibliographical references and index.
  ISBN 0-8020-4316-X (bound)   ISBN 0-8020-8141-X (pbk.)

  1. Frye, Northrop – Criticism and interpretation.   I. Title.

  PN75.F7C67 2000   801′.95   C00-931371-0

The financial support of the Social Sciences and Humanities Research
Council of Canada is gratefully acknowledged by the author.

This book has been published with the help of a grant from the Humanities
and Social Sciences Federation of Canada, using funds provided by the
Social Sciences and Humanities Research Council of Canada.

University of Toronto Press acknowledges the financial assistance to its
publishing program of the Canada Council for the Arts and the Ontario
Arts Council.

University of Toronto Press acknowledges the financial support for its
publishing activities of the Government of Canada through the Book
Publishing Industry Development Program (BPIDP).

To the patient and steady ones with my love and gratitude.

What do the poets 'say'?
They say that everything is everywhere at once.
They say that all nature is alive.
They say that all creation is dialectic, separating heaven
     and hell.
They say that the material world neither is nor isn't, but
     disappears.
They say that the created world neither is nor isn't, but appears.
They say that the containing form of real experience is myth.
They say that time and space are disappearing categories.
They say that men are Man, as gods are God.

(Northrop Frye, Notebook 18, par. 121)

Contents

Abbreviations

The following abbreviations are used in parenthetical references within the text.

AC   *Anatomy of Criticism: Four Essays.* Princeton UP, 1957.

CP   *The Critical Path: An Essay on the Social Context of Literary Criticism.* Bloomington: Indiana UP, 1971.

CR   *Creation and Recreation.* Toronto: U of Toronto P, 1980.

DV   *The Double Vision: Language and Meaning in Religion.* Toronto: U of Toronto P, 1991.

EAC   *The Eternal Act of Creation: Essays, 1979–1990.* Ed. Robert D. Denham. Bloomington: Indiana UP, 1993.

EI   *The Educated Imagination.* Toronto: CBC, 1963.

FI   *Fables of Identity: Studies in Poetic Mythology.* New York: Harcourt, Brace and World, 1963.

FS   *Fearful Symmetry: A Study of William Blake.* Princeton: Princeton UP, 1947.

GC   *The Great Code: The Bible and Literature.* New York: Harcourt Brace Jovanovich, 1982.

MC   *The Modern Century.* Toronto: Oxford UP, 1967.

MM   *Myth and Metaphor: Selected Essays, 1974–1988.* Ed. Robert D. Denham. Charlottesville: UP of Virginia, 1990.

NB   Notebook.

NFC   *Northrop Frye in Conversation.* Ed. David Cayley. Concord,
         ON: Anansi, 1992.

NFCL   *Northrop Frye on Culture and Literature: A Collection of Review Essays.* Ed. Robert D. Denham. Chicago: U of
         Chicago P, 1978.

NFHK   *The Correspondence of Northrop Frye and Helen Kemp, 1932–1939.* Ed. Robert D. Denham. 2 vols. Toronto: U of
         Toronto P, 1996.

NFR   *Northrop Frye on Religion: Excluding 'The Great Code' and
         'Words with Power.'* Ed. Alvin A. Lee and Jean O'Grady.
         Toronto: U of Toronto P, 2000.

NS   Giambattista Vico. *The New Science.* Abridged trans. Thomas Goddard and Max Harold Fisch. Ithaca, NY: Cornell
         UP, 1970.

SE   *Northrop Frye's Student Essays, 1932–1938.* Ed. Robert D.
         Denham. Toronto: U of Toronto P, 1997.

SeS   *The Secular Scripture: A Study of the Structure of Romance.*
         Cambridge, MA.: Harvard UP, 1976.

SM   *Spiritus Mundi: Essays on Literature, Myth, and Society.*
         Bloomington: Indiana UP, 1976.

StS   *The Stubborn Structure: Essays on Criticism and Society.*
         Ithaca, NY: Cornell UP, 1970.

WP   *Words with Power: Being a Second Study of 'The Bible and
         Literature.'* New York: Harcourt Brace Jovanovich, 1990.

WTC   *The Well-Tempered Critic.* Bloomington: Indiana UP, 1963.

NORTHROP FRYE
AND THE POETICS OF PROCESS

Introduction:

Beyond the Great Divide:
Frye and a Unified Theory
of Criticism

It has often been remarked that theorists of the sublime mirror their subject matter, invariably expressing themselves in a 'high style,' and we may recall here Boileau's observation that Longinus 'is himself the great sublime he draws' (Monk 22). In his comprehensive study of the English eighteenth-century sublime, Samuel Monk cites a passage from the 1809 *Elements of Art* by Martin Shree that puts an ironic slant on what had, by this time, become a commonplace of the sublime:

> those who talk rationally on other subjects no sooner touch on this, than they go off in a literary delirium; fancy themselves, like Longinus, 'the great sublime they draw,' and rave like Methodists, of inward lights, and enthusiastic emotions, which, if you cannot comprehend, you are set down as un-illumined by the grace of criticism, and excluded from the elect of Taste. (Monk 3)

In this study I focus on a thinker who spent the better part of his professional life pondering the sublimity of the structure of literature and literary language, while being, if not a 'raving Methodist,' then at least a self-avowed 'undercover-agent' for the United Church of Canada (*DV* xiii).

Like Longinus before him, though often in less flattering terms, Northrop Frye has been found to adopt an 'elevated' critical stance. Barbara Herrnstein Smith, to name one of a raft of like-minded commentators, views Frye as an unselfconscious humanist who is trapped in a 'double-discourse of value' that privileges the elevated and sublime while insisting that value judgments have no place in literary criticism (*Contingencies of Value* 17–29).[1] There can be no question that Frye's own centre of literary interest tends to gravitate towards the established English canon (Shakespeare, Milton), but we should also recall that Frye's first major publication, *Fearful Symmetry*, represents nothing less than a frontal attack on the received canon of the day and that it was precisely this text that sparked the flurry of critical interest in Blake that continues to this day.[2] Frye's own individual literary preferences and critical preoccupations have nothing to do, however, with his main thesis, regrettably and consistently misinterpreted, that the function of a critic is not to reject any given literary work but to recognize it for what it is and to understand it in relation to other works within the 'order of words,' that is, the entire body of literature (*MM* 140).

We live, it is said, in an age of rampant scepticism, or, in Vichian terms, in a radically ironic age which inevitably transforms any 'loftiness' of tone and ideology into parody and satire. Because we may be seen to be of an age at the furthest remove from the sublime, it is understandable that Frye's elevated tone, like his liberal-humanist ethos, would fail to strike a chord. And yet, despite Frank Lentricchia's oft-quoted relegation of Frye to the dustbin of literary criticism (30), the concrete indications are (as Robert Denham has carefully documented) that Frye's influence, like the sublime itself, evinces a tenacity that should not be disregarded.[3]

Despite ongoing distaste for the sublime with its lingering taint of the metaphysical, the mystical, and the transcendent, even a cursory review of current critical theory reveals that the sublime has, in fact, again become an important focus for critical discourse.[4] In addition, there is a profound conceptual affinity between the currently widespread relativistic stance espoused by critics like Barbara Herrnstein Smith and the Vichian constructivism that subtends Frye's critical endeavours, a constructivism which Lentricchia's dismissive 'aestheticism' does not adequately confront (25).

Frye's work, like that of Wittgenstein and Adorno in this century, and of Vico in an earlier one, represents a severe interrogation of rationalism and Cartesian thought. The common thread in these investigations is the notion of the incommensurability of matter and concept. As Jean-François Lyotard has outlined, there have emerged today out of this philosophical stance two powerful and quite divergent critical tendencies. One of these entails a sense of powerlessness, of melancholy and regret for a lost presence; in contrast to this, the second involves a focus on the empowered and unanchored word, the confident celebration of possibility and conceivability, of '*novatio*' and 'assay' (*The Postmodern Condition* 80). That this schism represents a crisis for contemporary thought has been repeatedly noted not only by Frye but by many other contemporary critical thinkers as well.[5] It is precisely around the concept of the sublime that Frye and other critical thinkers have been circling in an attempt to confront this source of mounting critical anxiety, an anxiety reminiscent of the 'nihilistic psychosis' captured by Blake in *Jerusalem* and which, as Frye notes in his 1969 preface to *Fearful Symmetry,* again holds us in its grip.

The contours of Frye's critical engagements, from those early explorations of Blake's fearful symmetries (1947) to the final *tour de force* of the commonplaces of the sublime that is *Words with Power* (1990), are circumscribed by the Longinian problematic of 'elevation,' that certain quality which, for Longinus, marked 'greatness' in a literary work. As will be discussed below, Vico's precocious eighteenth-century insights into the historical and philosophical primacy of mythopoeic, metaphorical language represent important critical analogues and precedents for Frye's explorations of the nature, functions, and implications of 'elevated' language in human life. This postulate of a Vichian rather than a Kantian or Burkean slant to Frye's Longinianism necessarily requires significant elaboration. Like Vico, and in marked contrast to Kant, Frye gives epistemological privilege to *oratio* over *ratio* and *verbum* over *res*. In the case of Edmund Burke, with whom there are notable affinities, significant incongruencies serve to highlight innovations by Frye that represent a major shift in the theory of the sublime. A primary concern of this project is to

demonstrate that, in his expansion of the Longinian critical tradition into an aesthetics of process, in contradistinction to the
Aristotelian paradigm based on the aesthetic product, Frye manages to temper and correct the misogynistic privileging of a negative and terrible sublime (the sublime of the Father) which had
dominated the tradition from at least the eighteenth century,
although the seeds of this aesthetic take us back to the very roots
of patriarchy and of monotheism.

Despite Croce's insistent proclamation that the sublime is a
moribund aesthetic (Russo 9) and Hegel's similar rejection of the
sublime as a merely 'affective and subjective phenomenon' (Fry
193), we see today an extension of theories of the sublime into the
central ring of critical discourse where it is being confronted by a
broad range of historical, political, social, and ethical challenges.[6]
In a postmetaphysical age defined by what Gianni Vattimo has
described in *La fine della modernità* as 'the destruction of the idea
of truth and of foundations' as well as the relinquishment of the
ideal of progress (176), Frye's insistence on the visionary power of
mythopoeic language, on the constructive capacities of literary
illusion, represents a faith in, and a commitment to, the positive
and liberating dimensions of such seemingly pessimistic postu-
lates.[7] Indeed, these hallmarks of contemporary thought may be
viewed as the very culmination or consequence of the project of
aesthetics, engaged as it has been from its inception in the attempt to 'achieve a judicious reinsertion of the body into a dan-
gerously abstract discourse' (Eagleton 337).

The increasingly valorized aspect of metaphorical thinking that
has been variously described as 'primitive,' 'aboriginal,' and 'corporeal' is centrally implicated in Frye's expanded poetics of the
sublime, for it is the experiential pivot around which Frye's main
lines of inquiry revolve. For Frye, the cultivation of intensity of
consciousness through the epiphanic, or 'radical' metaphorical
language of poetry serves to counteract that distancing self-reflex-
ivity and anxious alienation of humanity from the realm of the
natural and material world which analytical and abstract reasoning entails. It represents, furthermore, the means by which the
free existential play with nature, of which human nature is capa-

ble, may take place. As we may experience, for example, on reading Emily Dickinson's 'I saw no way –' or Leopardi's 'L'infinito,' this type of metaphor-induced *ecstasis* involves the *mise en abîme* of a mind and a world alternately experienced as possessed and possessing, containing and contained, identical and different. It is this experience that fuels the vertigo of the sublime response. What is entailed is *not* a sublimation or displacement of psychic energies, but rather a clearing away of the clutter of history in order that a direct and intense apprehension of the experience of living may break through. The primordial, metaphor-making habit of mind that is preserved in literary language ensures that in an era increasingly preoccupied with difference, *différance*, deconstruction, and destruction, the ability to contrive identities, unities, and syntheses, without thereby eradicating variety and discreteness, remains tenable. This type of radically metaphorical identification also represents the experiential mode in which the epistemological crisis or *agon* of human being is most economically and powerfully proclaimed and suffered in the impertinent disjunction of metaphor's paradoxical is and is not, in the simultaneous experience of sense and dissonance that metaphor offers.

Northrop Frye was a literary critic and theorist who caused a great deal of grief for a great number of literary scholars, as a review of secondary sources on Frye immediately reveals.[8] The critiques tend to fall into two main groups, although the permutations and combinations that have emerged are, in themselves, quite intriguing. Some tend to react to Frye's proposal that criticism is to be considered a 'coherent and comprehensive theory of literature, logically and scientifically organized' by 'systematic and progressive' research into a 'unified structure of knowledge' which studies literature much as physics is an organized body of knowledge that studies nature (*AC* 11). Like nature, literature is a productive power that cannot speak about itself, but rather must be conceptually reconstructed through critical attention, much as history reconstructs human action and the physical sciences make progressive stabs at describing nature (*AC* 12). Frye's call for a criticism that is, 'scientific,' that is, a structured and progressive accumulation of knowledge about literature in which there is no

place for value judgments, has led some critics, like Geoffrey
Hartman, to conclude that, although Frye's is a worthy attempt to
'demystify and democratize the muse' (110), it is hampered in its
attempt to reach a wide audience by its very emphasis on 'system'
(131), by its compulsion to account for and accommodate a vast
assortment of verbal forms into an ordered synchronic unity while
disregarding the question of time and history (122).

On the other hand, Frye has also drawn forth critiques from
those who see in his 'schematics' and 'neutral anatomizing'
(Krieger, *Northrop Frye in Modern Criticism* 5) attempts to detach
literature from the world of reality (Hirsch, *The Aims of Interpretation* 95–6) and to deflect criticism from the task of evaluation
(Wimsatt 80). Furthermore, according to Wimsatt, the genuine
and ideal society ostensibly promoted by literature is really, for
Frye, nothing but an empty dream, while the tortured distinction
between the imaginative and the imaginary fails to stand up to
scrutiny (81; Graff, *Poetic Statement and Critical Dogma* 69–78). In a
veritable flood of negativity, Wimsatt goes on to chastise Frye for
his undiscriminating catholicity of 'interest' and for his failure to
adequately comment on the direct experience of the individual
literary work as representing the centre of criticism (82), a concern shared by Murray Krieger (1964) and the critic Ihab Hassan
(1964), *inter alia.* René Wellek pushes this point even further, for
he claims that Frye 'spins his fancies in total disregard of the text
and even builds fictional universes ... His criticism is an elaborate
fiction which loses all relation to knowledge, science, and concept' (257). E.D. Hirsch, like Barbara Herrnstein Smith, finds
Frye's élitism to reside in his bias in favour of the non-referential
language of literature, in his dualizing habit of mind that dis-
misses as secondary any discourse but the centripetal verbal structures of the mythopoeic (1967); he also takes Frye to task for his
dismissal of value judgments and for his alleged disregard of the
social context of criticism (95–6), an accusation echoed by
Lentricchia (229–31) and by John Fekete (1977).

As this brief, very partial overview suggests, Frye has elicited
negative appraisals from the entire spectrum of the critical estab-
lishment. For structuralists and materialists Frye is not rigorous

and scientific enough, not sufficiently grounded in history, fact, and world, while to those of a more romantic or psychological perspective he is to be faulted for a pedantic, universalizing, and abstractive system-building project that has little to do with the actual experience of reading literature.

That Frye's critical endeavours can accommodate such divergent critiques is a testimony to a quality which certain very careful readers of Frye have variously called Frye's 'synoptic' (Hamilton 15) or 'synchretic' (Denham, *Northrop Frye and Critical Method* 32), encyclopaedic, and metacritical approach to the subject of criticism. The shortcomings of the parsimonious views mentioned above, and of countless others offered in a similar vein, are reducible to a failure to concede that for Frye, criticism rests on a radical awareness of language (*AC* 354; *MM* 129; *WP* 27) and that language is an inherently variable, complex phenomenon, serving a multitude of masters and adopting myriad discursive strategies. If rigorous examination of the ways of language is a key goal of the critical path, and for Frye this is certainly so, it is self-evident that all structured verbal entities may be seen to come under the purview of criticism and that the heuristic assumption of coherence or order for these words must be adopted if they are to be susceptible to inductive survey and collective scrutiny.

Frye's emphasis on language as a structuring vehicle is certainly not anomalous in the context of contemporary criticism; we see the same emphasis in phenomenologists, Heideggerians, and Lacanians, while the privileged place of *oratio* or rhetoric over *ratio* or logic brings Frye, in this sense, very close to Derrida and the deconstructionists (Hamilton 217–18) as well as to reception theory and discourse analysis.[9] This task of attempting to integrate the various languages of criticism into a 'conspectus of literature' via what Frye calls the formulation of a *theoria* rather than a theory (*AC* 348; 'Auguries of Experience' 2) encompasses a militantly reconciliatory agenda, one that refuses to concede that critical methodology may not encompass both rationalist, structuralist, or scientific approaches *and* the visionary, prophetic, ecstatic, and oracular aspects of verbal semiosis. Indeed, Frye is insistent that both *must* find a place in critical theory, for they both arise in, and are called for by, linguistic and literary phenomena themselves. It would thus be a patent omission to posit a critical theory based on the exclusion of either (*AC* 62). So, too, would it be foolhardy to ignore the fact that the centripetal impulse of language and literature and the radical intertextuality and self-consciousness of certain verbal structures do not preclude the overwhelmingly centrifugal direction of meaning and concern taken by other, more 'transparent' linguistic constructs. The entire range of semantic experience that words potentially offer must be counted in and accounted for by a *theoria* of criticism. And, despite Lubomir Doležel's observation that Frye's system, as set forth in the *Anatomy*, constitutes a 'poetics' because of its epistemological assumptions (181), it is understandable that Frye, arguing precisely for a critical theory that encompasses both Aristotelian and Longinian traditions, would eschew a term conventionally associated with the former tradition and often dismissive of the latter, as Doležel's own survey of occidental poetics reinforces.

Although the *Anatomy* does attempt to take an over-arching and wide-angled view of literary criticism, it makes no gesture towards the closure of reification. On the contrary, an examination of the definition of 'anatomy' in the *Anatomy* underscores the heuristic, explanatory, hospitable nature of Frye's critical enterprise, the fact that it is an attempt to suggest the unity and coherence of the skeleton or structure of criticism while leaving ample space for bodily growth and change.

The challenge for criticism in the present era is, as Frye stated with unambiguous emphasis in the 1957 conclusion to *Anatomy of Criticism*, precisely the reconciliatory agenda of 'reforging the broken links between creation and knowledge, art and science, myth and concept' (354). That this agenda represents a renewal of the task undertaken some two hundred years earlier by Giambattista Vico in his attempt to posit such a unified theory of culture is offered as a key point of departure for this study. It is my intention to explore the close affinities between the ideas of Frye and of Vico and to extrapolate some of the implications of these affinities for critical theory and, in particular, for the poetics of sublimity. This is a branch of critical theory that Frye called the 'aesthetics of process' in an early and seminal essay entitled 'To-wards Defining an Age of Sensibility,' later incorporated in modi-fied form in *Anatomy of Criticism* and considerably expanded upon in *The Well-Tempered Critic* (1963).[10]

We may regard Frye's career as critic and critical theorist as a perpetual criss-crossing of the discursive space of critical engage-ments. He moves from the intense, exacting study of individual authors (Blake, Milton, Shakespeare) to an engagement with the dizzying yet discrete expanse of critical theory itself (*Anatomy of Criticism*, *The Well-Tempered Critic*); from a concern with the social function of criticism and literature (*The Critical Path*, *The Educated Imagination*) to an examination of the links between language, history, culture, and religion (*The Great Code*, *The Double Vision*), all the while insisting, implicitly and explicitly, on the multiplicity, complexity, and centrality of the critical task. In his 'Letter to the English Institute' of 1965, Frye noted that criticism has nothing to do with rejection (thus his scorn for the subjectivism and vacilla-tions of personal and collective tastes) but only with recognition (29). And the most fundamental recognition to be made in criti-cism is that the study of literature breaks down into two essential categories: the study of literature as an object of knowledge, as a product; and the study of literature as experience, as process.

Critics have noted Frye's predilection for spatial metaphors in conceptualization but it is often overlooked that these metaphors imply not a static, fossilized, mental segmentation, but rather a relational, mobile, and dynamic constructive enterprise.[11] Frye presents us with a critical universe that is alive with the multi-directional movement of ideas, relationships, and 'interpenetra-tions,' to use one of Frye's favourite and philosophically loaded images. The critical configuration of literature as process and as product is no less dynamic in its formulation than are other of Frye's schematizations, with perhaps the most notable being the bidirectional spiralling spin of centre and circumference. A.C. Hamilton, one of Frye's most assiduous and close readers, has described the holistic feedback loop that may be seen to unify the distinction between literature as experience and literature as knowl-edge when he notes that Frye argues that criticism begins when reading ends: no longer imaginatively subjected to a literary work, the critic tries to make sense out of it, not by going to some historical context or by commenting on the immediate experience of reading but by seeing its structure within literature and literature within culture. As his argument develops, however, he reverses his order: a fully imaginative response may begin only after criticism ends (27).

That Frye is seeking to undermine any simple and tidy distinction between art and science in his conception of criticism is a conclusion also arrived at by Hazard Adams; Adams notes that *Anatomy* turns itself outside-in, proceeding from the declaration that criticism is to be scientific to identifying criticism with art and even positing a literary genre, anatomy, in which this work of criticism is itself to be placed in a telling use of *mise en abîme* techniques (41). Frye himself has noted that he thinks metaphorically, like poets (*NFC* 9, 13, 30), while he insists in one of the essays of *Divisions on a Ground* entitled 'Teaching the Humanities Today' that

> In the study of language and literature the scholarly aspect of the human mind is struggling with the creative aspect ... The scholar is concerned with the continuous accumulation of knowledge, yet all the time there is an underlying drive towards a more continuous kind of wisdom, an insight for which all knowledge is only a symbol and literature itself a means. (101)

It is not surprising, then, to find commentators noting that 'Frye's criticism has endured because of its rhetorical power' and that it does not rest exclusively on its 'explanatory power and discursive good sense' (Denham, 'Auguries of Influence' 88). In Frye's cultivated wit and elegance, in his pithiness and economy of expression, in the compelling and suggestive architectonics of texts such as *Anatomy* and *The Great Code*, and in the tendency towards aphorism, epiphany, and the oracular, we may indeed find proof of Frye's contention that critical writing need not necessarily be 'sub-creative' (*SM* 105).[12]

It would seem, then, that Frye is not, ultimately, so very far removed from the critic Ihab Hassan: Frye too is content to have the distinction between literature as experience and literature as knowledge occasionally blur. Like Hassan, Frye chose a life in literary criticism in order to be 'in the vicinity of that joy' (Hassan, 'Confessions of a Reluctant Critic' 14) which should only be intensified, not diluted, by critical knowledge. The end of literary education, like the end of literature itself, entails, for Frye, a heightening of mental experience, which is one way of achieving the state of being fully alive, fully awake, fully engaged in the rapture of the world's being and in the fact of being, now, in the world (*SeS* 161; *WTC* 142; *WP* 28). And, although critics of the either/or schools with their foreshortened focus have tended to see the presence of oracular elements and epiphanies in Frye's own scholarly, 'teacherly' texts as impractical and dated fictions,[13] a mere step or two back will reveal, from the expansiveness of the both/and stance, that these moments represent the appropriate culmination of Frye's reconciliatory critical agenda. In Vichian terms, we may look upon Frye as his own best exemplar of how, in a late ironic age, the poetry of criticism may flourish, how the sublimity of metaphor may overlap and coexist with the implosive bathos of irony, how critical commentary may be centripetal and structuralistic while also being centrifugal and engaged in the broader concerns of culture and society. Frye's *œuvre* is a truly ambitious attempt to delineate the shape of a 'contrapuntal' criticism[14] which encompasses both the rationalistic and the oracular extremes of human intellection within its play; an attempt to recover the wholeness of what Julian Jaynes has explored as the 'bicameral mind.' What Frye sought and what he largely succeeded in tracing, was, as he wrote in 1963, 'a more unified conception of criticism ... an approach that does not try to split up the mind, or ignore the obvious fact that both intellect and emotion are fully and simultaneously involved in all our literary experience' (*WTC* 144).

The Maze in the Woods and the Guide

Frye makes the observation in an as yet unpublished notebook (NB 19, par. 379) composed during 1964 and 1965 that it is almost

impossible to believe that William Blake had not read Vico.[15] He
goes on to observe that of course he had not, which makes the
exploration of the affinities between these two towering eighteenth-century intellects particularly compelling in view of the
pivotal role they have assumed in shaping the critical and ideological principles of Frye. The extent of their influence on Frye
has been duly noted and commented upon, although the connection to Vico has been accorded considerably less scrutiny. Denham's
1987 bibliography offers, for example, fifty-nine indexical entries
under 'Blake' but only eight for 'Vico.'[16]

Frye has himself repeatedly acknowledged the immensity of his
debt to Blake, a debt reflected in the ten years spent in the
composition and revision of *Fearful Symmetry*, Frye's first book-
length publication and a major event in Blake criticism.[17] Frye
said to David Cayley, for example, that it was Blake who opened
his eyes to the mythological frame of our culture (*NFC* 47), while
in *Stubborn Structure* he wrote that all his critical ideas had been
derived from his study of Blake and that therefore *Anatomy* was
contained 'in embryo' in *Fearful Symmetry* (160). A.C. Hamilton
has compiled a list of what he deems to be the four key areas of
influence exerted on Frye by Blake (38–9). These are: Blake as
'guru,' 'spiritual preceptor,' or 'oracular revealer of mysteries' (*FS*
426); Blake as conduit to the subject of literary theory (*SM* 16; *CP*
14); Blake as source of the principle that the 'Old and New
Testaments are the Great Code of Art'; and finally, Blake as the
source of the crucial insight that poetic thought is 'inherently
schematic' and that thus 'criticism must be so too' (*StS* 176; cf.
Frye and Modern Criticism 28; *SM* 247). This list effectively, if unin-
tentionally, highlights crucial aspects of Frye's critical preoccupations that eventually land him squarely within the critical space of
the sublime. This point, which will be accorded substantial expansion below, should not be at all surprising, for Blake was himself a
key though late player in what stands to date as the most effusive
and fertile period of Longinianism in England, the eighteenth
century.[18]

Frye's acknowledgments of Vico's influence are, if somewhat
inconsistent, just as emphatic, particularly during the second half

of his career. There is no mention of Giambattista Vico in *Fearful Symmetry*, and among Frye's published papers the earliest explicit reference to Vico so far uncovered takes us back to a 1946 review article entitled 'Turning New Leaves,' where, in the process of reviewing *Faith and History* by Reinhold Niebuhr and *Meaning in History* by Karl Löwith for the *Canadian Forum*, he discusses the cyclical views of history of Vico, Spengler, and Toynbee.[19] Frye also gives general indications as to his initial encounters with Vico when he states in the somewhat autobiographical essay 'Expanding Eyes' that Vico came into his reading after Spengler, who, together with Frazer, was a culture hero from his student days (*SM* 111, 113).

Among Frye's private papers, Robert Denham has, to date, found the earliest reference to Vico in a 1935 or 1936 student paper entitled 'The Augustinian Interpretation of History,' written for Professor Kenneth H. Cousland (*SE* 191–216). Denham has noted that although Vico is not cited in the bibliography of this paper, there are listed several books on social and political thinkers which may have contained discussions of Vico. We may conclude, then, that Frye was aware of Vico as early as the mid-1930s, even though, as he tells us, he did not actually read Vico until years later. Given that the English translation of the *New Science* did not appear until 1948 and was preceded only four years earlier by the publication of the English translation of *The Autobiography of Giambattista Vico* (1944), it is probably safe to assume that during the late 1940s and early 1950s Frye's knowledge of the substance of Vico's thought, particularly given the Vichian strains in James Joyce and Ernst Cassirer, would have notably increased.[20]

References to Vico in Frye's published essays during the 1950s and 1960s do not meaningfully increase in frequency, and Denham's bibliography reflects this when we note the time span between the first and second indexical references to Vico (a gap of twenty-six years). My own search suggests that some eleven years elapsed between the first and second explicit references to Vico in Frye's published work. *Anatomy of Criticism*, published in 1957, has, despite the Vichian outline of the first essay on the theory of modes, only one explicit, if oblique, reference to Vico, and that is found in the context of a discussion of Joyce and his 'Viconian theory of history' (62). Another early and oblique reference to Vico that also emerges in the context of a discussion of Joyce and his cyclical notion of history is found in the 1957 essay entitled 'Quest and Cycle in *Finnegans Wake*' (*FI* 256–65).

This paucity of direct published reference to Vico is intriguing for several reasons. There is, to begin with, Frye's own curious inconsistency with respect to his debt to Vico. We see that in *The Great Code* (1982) Frye states that although Vico's theory of linguistic modes was his point of departure, there was 'very little left of Vico' in 'what finally emerged' (5). He proceeds then to state that Vico's influence was 'more pronounced in *Anatomy of Criticism*' (1957), a text which, however, does not include the name 'Giambattista Vico' in its index and, as we have noted, contains only one brief mention of the name in the body of the text. More recently Frye stated without equivocation in *Words with Power* (1990) that *The Great Code* owed a good deal to Vico (xii).

This apparent uncertainty or inconclusiveness demonstrated by Frye in his own assessments of the locus of Vico's influence, together with the limited explicit public reference to Vico before the 1970s, does not seem at all in line with the frequency and nature of the privately recorded memos on Vico. In the 1964–5 notebook already mentioned (Notebook 19), in which Frye toyed with the contents of the 'Third Book,' that is, the one which was to follow *Anatomy*, fourteen specific references to Vico have been located. Given that *The Great Code* (1981) is the 'Third [big] Book' that eventually did emerge, it is helpful to note comments such as the following recorded in the much earlier notebook:

> I was thinking of a series of (somewhat melodramatic) titles for chapters. One, The Maze in the Wood; Two, The Finding of the Guide, who for this book is probably Vico. (NB 19, par. 359)

We may conclude that Frye had by this time, the mid-1960s, read portions, if not the entirety of *The New Science*, for he states: 'Vico, of whom I still have to make a long summary, says that the early wandering giants were frightened by the thunder into grabbing one woman and hauling her into a cave" (NB 19, par. 381). What also emerges from this notebook is the powerful link established between Vico as guide and the 'maze-in-the-wood' that is criticism. Still with reference to the 'Third Book' the notebook reads:

> Tentative plan: One: An introductory, or maze-in-the-wood chapter, posing the problem of the total subject csm. [criticism] belongs to, why it isn't lit. [literature], & the place of myth as the centre of concern. Vico probably has to come here. (NB 19, par. 366)

Further along, discussing the tripartite plan of the project, Frye proposes that

> The introduction, which outlines the whole scheme, also does the job of externalizing criticism, establishing its context & the kind of importance it could have if critics knew what they were talking about. This is the maze in the wood, the finding of the guide (Vico mainly) and the breaking of the branch. (NB 19, par. 399)

This persistent identification of Vico by way of images associated irrevocably with Dante, and Dante's own guide, Virgil, would strongly suggest that Frye was aware of Croce's controversial reassessment of Vico as the first thinker to really understand Dante. But it is with the publication of *The Critical Path* in 1970 that the public face is tentatively put on these private musings and we encounter in print the now familiar Dantesque images, intertexts, and metaphors from the notebook:

> About twenty-five years ago, when still in middle life, I lost my way in the dark wood of Blake's prophecies and looked around for some path that would get me out of there ... The critical path I wanted was a theory of criticism which would, first, account for the major phenomena of literary experience, and, second, would [*sic*] lead to some view of the place of literature in civilization as a whole. (13–14)

Although there is limited explicit use made of Vico in this text – only four specific references – the shadow of Vico haunts the entire project. A statement acknowledging Frye's expanded appreciation of the Neapolitan thinker's potential worth is, moreover, finally unconditionally offered:

> The conventions, genres and archetypes of literature do not simply appear: they must develop historically from origins, or perhaps from a common origin. In pursuing this line of thought, I have turned repeatedly to Vico, one of the very few thinkers to understand anything of the historical role of the poetic impulse in civilization as a whole. Vico describes how a society, in its earliest phase, sets up a framework of mythology, out of which all its verbal culture grows, including its literature. (34)[21]

In Vico, Frye found the critical thinker who would point towards a method for dealing with both key requirements that Frye demanded of critical theory: the ability to account for the 'major phenomena of literary experience' and the positing of a 'view of the place of literature in civilization as a whole' (CP 14). In other words, a theory of criticism that is centripetal as well as centrifugal, structuralistic and poststructuralistic, formal and yet aware of social context, rationalistic yet prepared to engage the fact of the extra-rational in literary language and experience.

In this present study, in contrast to the majority of in-depth analyses of Frye's work undertaken to date, the critical propositions of *Anatomy of Criticism*, gleaned in large part from Frye's work on his first guide, Blake, will represent not the end, but the beginning, the point of departure for what, it will be argued, is the mature statement of Frye's critical theories. This final elaboration, contained in the works of Frye's last two decades of production, represents a major achievement in critical theory, wherein the reconciliatory, encyclopaedic, and synchretic reach achieves its most philosophically cogent formulation on the basis of Vichian epistemological principles. These principles prompt from within their orbit not only a poetics, taken in the broad sense given to the term in *Anatomy* as 'a theory of criticism whose principles apply to the whole of literature and account for every valid type of critical procedure' (14), but also, and perhaps more importantly from

Frye's perspective, an ethics. This ethical component is profoundly linked to the second major tradition that Frye deems to be operative in the history of Western critical theory, namely the Longinian tradition that is concerned with literature as 'process' or experience rather than as product. Furthermore, it is my contention that with *Anatomy* Frye considered that his contribution to the Aristotelian strain in criticism, that is, to structural poetics – an expression which was, by the way, his original title for what eventually emerged as *Anatomy of Criticism* (Ayre 252) – had been substantially made and it was the psychological and social dimensions of literary experience that required further extensive critical attention.

The two central points of reference for my own study are topics in Frye criticism that have not received deserved and close scrutiny.[22] In attempting to correct this imbalance in Frye criticism by focusing primarily on the affinities between Vico and Frye in the first place, and in the second place, on Frye's related efforts to articulate a poetics of process, I have elected to proceed thematically rather than chronologically. This decision was founded on two primary considerations: it will allow for a more streamlined, coherent, and less repetitive presentation of my arguments, while also permitting me to take cognizance of, and act on, Frye's frequently made observation that his thought proceeds by dialectical expansion rather than by linear progression in time. Moreover, such a *modus operandi* is suggested by the fact that with respect to both the Vichian and the Longinian content in Frye, the later major publications, namely, *The Great Code* and *Words with Power*, together with the essays produced during the same period, constitute an important focus for this inquiry primarily in their interplay with, and expansion from, *Anatomy*.

one

Process, the Sublime, and the Eighteenth Century

When we observe that two of Frye's intellectual predecessors and, as he would have it, 'guides,' William Blake and Giambattista Vico, emerged out of the intellectual turbulence of the eighteenth century, it should not come as a surprise that, for Frye, this period came to occupy a special place in the history of Western thought. Because of the profound changes in the mythological thinking of this era, Frye saw it as a threshold between modernity and pre-modernity. In the third Whidden Lecture, delivered at Mc-Master University in 1967, Frye gave a summary of this transition saying:

> It seems to me that there have been two primary mythological contributions in Western culture. One was the vast synthesis that institutionalized Christianity made of its Biblical and Aristotelian sources ... The other is the modern mythology that began when the modern world did, in the later eighteenth century. (*MC* 106–7)

The crucial paradigm shift which characterized this cross-over was a consequence of developments in philosophy which we now associate primarily with Giambattista Vico, but which Frye encountered early in his career in William Blake. At the core of these developments is the conviction that human civilization is indeed humanly created (*MC* 109). In treating this topic in his *Study of English Romanticism* (1968), Frye writes:

Gradually, at first, in such relatively isolated thinkers as Vico, then more confidently, the conviction grows that a great deal of all this creative activity ascribed to God is projected from man, that man has created the forms of his civilization, including his laws and his myths, and that consequently they exhibit human imperfection. (14)

This revolutionary proposition emerged out of the compulsion of the age of reason to investigate origins and first causes. Frank Manuel suggests in *The Eighteenth Century Confronts the Gods* that there was a child-like curiosity and a naive belief among eighteenth-century investigators that only by reconstructing the 'primitive mind' would access be had to an understanding of the emergence of civil life, that is, the emergence of language, of social organization, and of religious institutions and mores (132). It was when the age of reason directed its analytical eye to scrutinize the nature and origins of religion (particularly given the abundance of descriptive data concerning 'pagan' beliefs and practices made available as a result of European mercantile and missionary expansion) that the human emotions emerged as a key focus for gaining an understanding of distinctively human behaviour. Despite the necessary cautious qualifications, and the careful distinctions initially made between pagan monotheism and Judaeo-Christian doctrines, the hypothesis was eventually formulated that 'religious sentiment was not inborn, but was acquired by men at a given moment in time ...' (Manuel 134). Manuel traces the roots of this hypothesis back through Hobbes to the pre-Socratics who posited naturalistic interpretations of the worship of gods (36). According to these early thinkers, religious belief represented a defensive response triggered by the fear of death and the associated anxiety aroused by a nature perceived as hostile and threatening (143–4).

These considerations, and particularly the 'fear doctrine,' will receive considerable scrutiny below, especially in the course of discussing the ideas of Giambattista Vico and Edmund Burke. What is to be recognized at this juncture, though, is that the interest of the eighteenth-century critics in the sublime was part and parcel of this fascination with the human impetus towards religion that nature seemed to inspire in the primitive mind. John Dennis and Joseph Addison, for example, emphasized the religious basis of the pleasure inspired by qualities of grandeur and majesty in nature. In both we find a focus on the process of association or identification of nature with God, and for both the greatest sublime pleasure arises in the contemplation of the Divine (Albrecht 37–8).[1] In William Blake, in whose work we may discern the convergence of all the many elements of the sublime developed over the preceding century, there is an emphatic integration of world and spirit in what we may call an apocalyptic and hermeneutical sublime, one firmly grounded in language.[2]

This tendency for discussions of the sublime to approach the theological is present even in the early, pre-eminently stylistic, treatise of Longinus.[3] In discussing the first of his five sources of sublimity, nobility of soul, he refers to Homer and states, 'But far superior to the passages on the Battle of the Gods are those which represent the divine nature as it really is, pure, majestic, and undefiled' (111). The author then proceeds to give as examples a composite description of Poseidon from the *Iliad*, and the 'Let there be light' passage from Genesis.

Marjorie Hope Nicolson has minutely examined the key developments in seventeenth- and eighteenth-century thought that led to the unravelling or unmasking of this process whereby the forces of nature were projected or sublimated into the figures of powerful divinities. In particular, she describes the reconfiguration of the cosmos which ensued after the pivotal geophysical discoveries of the seventeenth century were given considerable impetus by the invention of the telescope. In *Mountain Gloom and Mountain Glory* (1959), Nicolson, by focusing on changes in the conception of the earth's topography, and on the aesthetic responses to it, traces what she describes as the 'development of the aesthetics of the infinite.' This emerged when the awe and terror previously associated with an infinite and omnipotent deity were gradually transferred to the infinite space of the newly expanded cosmos, one which ravished the imagination with the possibility of countless other potential worlds (139).[4]

This transposition from a theological to a geophysical focus represents, in effect, the undoing of the psychic projection of the gods, or, in Manuel's words, the 'confronting' of the gods. Although this development may be seen as recentring the human psyche within a material or natural order, the feeling of alienation and belittlement before the majesty, dimension, and inscrutable mystery of the given world – a world no longer sublunary, and no longer contained within the fixity of a spiritualized heavenly realm, nor spatialized in a chain or order of being – was by no means obliterated (Nicolson 143). Furthermore, this radical reconfiguration in cosmology and the anthropological investigations into the religious impulses of early humanity could not but suggest the unsettling conclusion that the so-called laws of nature, that is, 'the rational design that nature reflects,' were, no less than laws of political, social, and economic organization, human projections, human creations (*MC* 110). No longer was the mind seen to be engaged in 'discovering' and 'mirroring' the fixed order, laws, and design of a divinely crafted physical and moral order; rather, civil life in all its myriad manifestations was seen to be a product of human self- and world-creation, while nature itself, increasingly, came to be seen as similarly engaged in the trial and error process of self-generation or autopoesis (110).

In *The Mirror and the Lamp*, M.H. Abrams examines this transition in conceptions of the mind and convincingly argues that the movement from the model of the mind as mirror of nature to that of the mind as a lamp illuminating the cosmos which characterized eighteenth- and early nineteenth-century thought was paralleled by a renewed interest in the sublime (74–7). Abrams describes in detail the convergence of the aesthetic inquiry into the ability of poetry to 'move,' and the philosophical investigations into the nature of the relationship between mind and matter which took place at this time. As Frye implicitly recognized, this point of convergence achieved its most explicit articulation in the work of the two eighteenth-century thinkers noted earlier, Giambattista Vico in Italy, and William Blake in England.

Much of Frye's discussion of Blake's 'case against Locke' in the early chapters of *Fearful Symmetry* focuses precisely on the eighteenth-century shifts in the philosophy of mind that have just been described. This book represents Frye's own early attempts to circumscribe a philosophical ground for literature. As Frye was later to discover, this ground had been explicitly mapped out by Vico in his *New Science*. In Blake and to some extent in Vico, what emerged was a re-elaboration of the conception of the Plotinian figure of the mind as an overflowing fountain and as a source of power which '"gives radiance out of its own store" to the objects of sense' (Abrams, 59).[5] In both Blake and Vico, the exploration of this creative power unfolded as a polemic against thinkers who rejected the epistemological function of the imagination, or, as Blake would have it, of 'vision,' and privileged instead analytical reason and logical deduction. Blake's case against Locke was a re-play of Vico's case against Descartes.[6] Thus, for Frye, Blake and Vico came to represent essentially the same principle, one which the Latin shorthand of *verum factum* has come to summarize.[7] In the 1987 essay entitled, 'Blake's Bible' Frye essentially restates Vico's formulation of the *verum factum* principle, the idea, that is, that truth or meaning is made, not perceived. He then proceeds to give this formulation a Blakean and theological twist, saying: 'in Blake ... God and creative man being the same thing, his apoca-lypse is neither a humanistic vision of a better future nor a show of fireworks put on by God ... It is the attaining of a divine and hu-man identity whose creative powers are entirely without limits' (*MM* 286). In a 1990 interview with David Cayley, Frye implicitly accepted that Blake's 'vision' represents a version of Vico's *verum factum*. For Blake, 'vision' refers to the human capacity to 'know' reality and experience it intensely through acts of human recreation.[8]

In *Fearful Symmetry*, Frye used Blake's distinction between the visionary 'Hallelujah-Chorus' perception of the sun and its more prosaic, rationalistic reception as a round shining disc or 'guinea-sun' in order to explore the ethical reasons for privileging the former mental mode of operation over the latter. Following Blake, Frye discerned that the rationalistic preference for the Lockean guinea-sun and the rejection of the reality of the Hallelujah-chorus sun were attempts to arrive at a consensus about the reality of the sun, a 'common denominator' independent of individual and particular experiences of it (*FS* 21). In Blake's rejection of this Lockean one-size-fits-all approach to the construction of meaning in the world, Frye sees the essential objection to rest on the issue of individual freedom of thought:

> Blake's objection to Locke is that he extends the involuntary action into the higher regions of the imagination and tries to make perceptive activity subconscious. Locke does not think of sight as the mind directing itself through the eye to the object. He thinks of it as an involuntary and haphazard image imprinted on the mind through the eye by the object. In this process the mind remains passive and receives impressions automatically. We see the guinea-sun automatically: seeing the Hallelujah-Chorus sun demands a voluntary and conscious imaginative effort; or rather, it demands an exuberantly active mind which will not be a quiescent blank slate. The imaginative mind, therefore, is the one which has realized its own freedom and understood that perception is self-development. (*FS* 22–3)

For Frye, the imaginative mind is an 'exuberantly active mind' which has 'realized its own freedom.' In this formulation we may plumb the depths of Frye's commitment to his vocation as teacher and critic of literature, his commitment to the husbanding of imagination and thereby to the advancement of freedom. This privileging of the role of imagination in human aspirations toward freedom is present, though sometimes obliquely so, in the eighteenth-century debates around the nature of human understanding and also in the discourses on the sublime. Although the book is yet to be written that examines the noteworthy fact that the age of the flowering of theories of the sublime was also the age, *par excellence*, of revolution, there can be no doubt that for Blake, Vico, and Frye, questions of culture and artistic production are profoundly linked to the realm of praxis, to the social and political forms of world-making.[9] For Frye, as for Vico, the recognition of the profound link between the operations of imagination and of social and political organization may be seen as the fundamental conviction underlying his dedication to, and philosophy of, education.

In his synoptic universe of critical engagement Frye accomplishes, with a few grand strokes, the reconciliation and accommo-

dation of both the mirror and lamp models of human intellection. Frye's work represents a determined confrontation with
humanity's double vision, and in Longinus we may discern the
first explicit critical attempt to anatomize this binocularity. This is
something that Frye recognized very early on in his critical career.
Predictably, Frye's first explicit discussion of Longinianism is
framed within the context of the eighteenth century, the period
when the broader implications of Longinus's treatise on literary
intensity were being harvested.

Frye wrote two essays specifically on the English eighteenth
century. The first paper, which emerged during the first phase of
his career, is the 1956 essay entitled 'Towards Defining an Age of
Sensibility' (rpt. *FI* 130–7). As the title suggests, this piece focuses
primarily on the developments which tend to be associated with
the latter part of the century. The second essay, written some
thirty-four years later, 'Varieties of Eighteenth-Century Sensibility'
(1990), is instead concerned with the transitions that take place
within the eighteenth century itself, rather than with attempting
to describe the cultural threshold that the 'age of sensibility'
represents between the age of reason and that of romanticism. It
is the first of the two essays that is of crucial importance to Frye's
critical theories. This essay and the abridged and modified version
of it that was incorporated into the First Essay on modes in
Anatomy deserve to be closely scrutinized, for they delineate the
enclosing frame for all of Frye's critical models and suggest the
logic of continuity in the progression of Frye's work, from the
study of Blake, to *Anatomy of Criticism*, and culminating in the two
final ambitious and expansive studies of the Bible. They also
represent the key that allows us to entertain a new perspective on
Frye's place in the history of critical thought, one that situates
him within a long line of thinkers who go back not only, as has
been repeatedly suggested, to Aristotle, but also, and just as importantly, to Longinus.[10]

Although Frye nowhere set out to explicitly generate a treatise
on the sublime, by acknowledging Longinus's treatise and the
tradition in criticism that flowed from it, Frye was able to formulate a cogent theoretical model of literary criticism that is truly

comprehensive and synchretic in scope. Frye's critical universe not only embraces the structuralistic aspects of the tradition that were initially mapped out by Aristotle, but also recognizes that there has developed, alongside this tradition, a complementary one concerned with the other variables outside of the text that are implicated in the literary process – namely, the reader, the author, and the world.

It is ironic that, although Frye's scholarly enterprise is embedded in the study of literary subjects conventionally associated with the sublime (Milton, Blake, the Bible), he has managed to avoid taking a direct and substantial approach to this complex and, of late, much discussed critical category.[11] Yet, although Frye failed to explicitly formulate a general theoretical model of the sublime, such a model is implicit in, and permeates much of, his thought, and may in fact be seen as constitutive of the most fundamental distinctions that he draws in the history of literary theory and in literature itself. In the essay 'Towards Defining an Age of Sensibility,' Frye proposed that the history of literary theory is primarily characterized by the confrontation between Aristotelian and Longinian views of literature:

> [I]n the history of literature we become aware, not only of periods, but of a recurrent opposition of two views of literature. These two views are the Aristotelian and the Longinian, the aesthetic and the psychological, the view of literature as product and the view of literature as process. (*FI* 130–1)

In *Anatomy of Criticism*, published one year later in 1957, substantially the same formulation is reiterated; however, in a shift which has important implications for Frye's latent theory of the sublime and its connection to Vico and Blake, the word 'psychological' is replaced by the word 'creative' (*AC* 66). In the Aristotelian view, plot, or narrative, or the internal fiction, is of primary interest; in the Longinian perspective the focus is on the 'idea or poetic thought,' the theme, the 'conceptual interest' or, as Aristotle designated it, the *dianoia* (*AC* 52).

The fundamental contrast entailed by this division between the view of literature as aesthetic product and the view of literature as creative process rests, in large part, on the attitude of the reader or critic. In the Aristotelian or 'product' stance, the work is objectified: it is an artefact which the reader-critic dispassionately examines from a certain 'aesthetic distance' (66). Catharsis is, for Frye, the central conception of Aristotle's critical stance, and what catharsis implies is 'the detachment of the spectator, both from the work of art itself and from the author' (66).[12] Aesthetic apprehension thus inevitably implies emotional and intellectual detachment from the object and its creator.

It would be a mistake to conflate Frye's notion of catharsis with that of Aristotle (Denham, *Frye and Critical Method* 30). Frye makes it clear that he views this quality of detachment as being primarily applicable to fictional modes, that is, to those literary modes which stress plot or action. Frye therefore suggests that Aristotle intended to extend the notion of catharsis in other genres besides tragedy (*AC* 66). This is not clear on the face of the *Poetics* as we have received it. It is Frye who has explicitly related catharsis in all the fictional modes as being that quality of detachment from a literary work which marks a particular attitude of the reader-critic. This represents a substantial departure from the conventional and still predominant understanding of Aristotle's conception of catharsis as a purging of emotional disturbance.[13] Frye's considerable extension of the notion of catharsis emerges as particularly instrumental and convenient in allowing a juxtaposition to 'ecstasis,' the mind-set of the reader-critic in Frye's reconstruction of Longinus's critical approach.

In the Longinian or 'process' view of literature which Frye designates as 'creative' rather than 'aesthetic,' and which seems to adhere to the 'thematic' aspects of literature (that is, to those aspects which are less 'objective'), the relationship between author and reader, one which extends beyond the confines of the text, becomes more prominent (*AC* 66). Thus, while catharsis may involve the release of emotions (such as those of pity and fear in tragedy), in the Longinian approach the emotions are contained rather than purged; instead of being attached to the disassociated and distanced aesthetic product as qualities, the emotions are intensified in that response which, in being experienced, throws an existential circuit between author and reader through the medium of the text. Frye summarizes this key distinction between the Aristotelian and Longinian critical approaches saying

> Just as catharsis is the central conception of the Aristotelian approach to literature, so ecstasis or absorption is the central conception of the Longinian approach. This is a state of *identification* in which the reader, the poem, and sometimes, at least ideally, the poet also, are involved. (*AC* 67; my emphasis)

Frye explicitly associates the ecstasis of the Longinian critical focus with a state of identification between the reader, the poem, and, ideally, the poet. He then proceeds to observe that the Longinian conception is primarily that of a 'thematic' or 'individualized' response, more useful, generally, with lyrics, while the Aristotelian is more appropriate for plays. This is not, however, a hard and fast rule. We see, for example, that *Hamlet* is a play which leans to the thematic and which inspires psychological or emotional identification, and thus is more suitable for a Longinian critique. A dispassionate response is elicited instead by 'Lycidas,' which is a lyric 'with all passion spent' and thus is a more appropriate focus for Aristotelian critical principles (*AC* 67).

In the 1956 essay on the age of sensibility, Frye focused much of his attention on prose works which, he argued, fit within this category of process-centred texts. What emerged as distinctive for Frye in these texts was a persistent self-consciousness which made present to the reader the textual status of the object under scrutiny, evoking in the mind of the reader the process or act of creative composition and, thus, the presence of the author.[14] The most radical example offered is that of Sterne's *Tristram Shandy*, a text in which the reader is 'not being led into a story, but into the process of writing a story' (*FI* 131).[15] Similarly, where poetry emphasizes the original process of composition rather than the finished product, 'the qualities of subconscious association take the lead, and the poetry becomes hypnotically repetitive, oracular, incantatory, dreamlike and in the original sense of the word charming' (*FI* 133).

As the discussion of process in both *Anatomy* and the early paper on sensibility indicates, Frye conceived literary works themselves as tending towards either the process or the product stance, eliciting, by their very nature, one or the other of the two main critical perspectives on literature. Although he does not discuss intermediate texts, he certainly has not precluded the possibility that texts may contain appeals to, or accommodate, both perspectives. Furthermore, his discussion of the age of sensibility would suggest that at particular times and places, one or the other perspective may be seen to dominate the literary scene.

A.C. Hamilton has attempted to merge the two approaches, positing catharsis and ecstasis as phases within an ideal reading experience: 'Catharsis relates to the fictional modes as it brings the emotional detachment from a literary work which is the beginning of criticism; ecstasis relates to the thematic modes as it brings the imaginative involvement in the work which is the end of criticism' (77). Although there are works which may accommodate such a sequence of readerly responses – and the sequence may be *imposed* on any text – Hamilton does not draw sufficient attention to the fact that Frye's discussion is framed primarily as an either/or proposition. We also see Hamilton's tendency toward fusion in his curious, unsubstantiated observation that 'Aristotle's concept of catharsis, ... Frye consistently interprets in Longinian terms as the exhilaration a literary work arouses by its vision of a higher human state' (xiv). It is perhaps this refusal to take *at face value* Frye's clear distinction between Aristotelian and Longinian traditions that leads Hamilton to follow the established path and focus on the Aristotelian elements in Frye at the expense of the Longinian, and to disregard the entire question of the impact that the discourse on the sublime has had on Frye's notion of process in literature.

Frye's discussions of process literature and process criticism incorporate, if somewhat obliquely, some key eighteenth-century critical principles and debates which emerged in response to the revival of Longinus's treatise on the sublime.[16] This revival was principally indebted to Boileau's 1674 French translation of a text which, as Jules Brody has traced, had been in circulation in

Europe since its publication at Basel in 1554 by Francesco Robortello.[17] In the English eighteenth-century encounter with the sublime, on which Frye's discussion of process focuses, a particular direction emerged among the approaches to the sublime which was to impact profoundly on Immanuel Kant, and which proved determinative in the shaping of European romanticism and thus in establishing the bent of modernity.[18] That the epistemological tag of modernity should be linked to the question of sublimity need not surprise if it is remembered that the investigations of the sublime focused precisely on the 'response of the mind to the qualities and relations of objects in nature and in art' (Hipple 7).[19] The key philosophical node implicated in the development of the eighteenth-century sublime is one that juxtaposes analytical reason to creative imagination, the language of logic and deduction to the dizzying spirals of radically poetic, that is, metaphorical and mythical verbal constructs. This is a distinction which is at the foundation of Frye's own dichotomy between the Aristotelian and the Longinian styles of criticism and thus warrants considerable further scrutiny, for it represents the first key attribute of Frye's Longinianism – the epistemological privileging of the creative imagination over reason.

In both *Anatomy* and in the essay 'Towards Defining an Age of Sensibility,' Frye develops a taxonomy of the literature of process based on the emotions of fear and pity, and, in a tacit though somewhat contorted evocation of Edmund Burke's notion of the sublime experience as one premised on the psychological modes of terror and delight, he relegates the sublime to a subgroup of the process view of literature based on the psychological state of 'pleasurable fear without object' (Burke 39–40; *FI* 134–5; *AC* 66). This literature of process based on pleasurable fear without object, that is, sublime literature, is contrasted by Frye to literature of process based on *pity* without object in another indirect and twisted appropriation, in this case, of Burke's pivotal dichotomy, the sublime and the beautiful: 'we defined pity without an object as an imaginative animism which finds human qualities everywhere in nature, and includes the "beautiful," traditionally the corresponding term to the sublime' (*AC* 66; cf. *FI* 135).

Frye includes in his subcategories of 'process literature grounded in pity without object' the literature of 'apocalyptic exultation of all nature bursting into human life,' while the examples he gives are among those conventionally proffered as typical of sublime literature of the eighteenth century: namely, Smart's *Song to David*, the ninth night of *The Four Zoas*, and the *Songs of Experience*. It would seem that in the course of his taxonomic preoccupations, Frye has imposed a very narrow, Burkean scope on the word 'sublime.' In doing so, he has unnecessarily narrowed the theoretical or conceptual range of this term as it has manifested itself and evolved historically. As his observation that no term has ever been coined for 'pity without object' suggests, a historical argument may be made for the proposition that Frye's term 'literature of process' may be seen to incorporate various literary categories or kinds which have at various times in the past been classified under the rubric of 'sublime literature.' This conceptual move is very typical of recent criticism which displays a tendency to ignore the binarism of Burke's 'sublime and the beautiful' in favour of the binary oppositions which may be subsumed under or within the general genus of the 'sublime' (Ferguson, *Solitude and the Sublime* 69).

In Frye's critical system, this expanded, inclusive notion of the 'sublime' is renamed the category of 'process' and Burke's distinctions between sublimity and beauty, fear and pity, are subsumed within this broader category. By incorporating literature of heightened emotion into this one class or genus, and including within it the affective states of both fear *and* pity, Frye undercuts the axiological privilege of sublime fear over beauty and pity that had achieved dominance with Burke. Frye's notion of process literature, with its subsidiary discrimination between fear and pity, points to a strongly Blakean Longinian poetics which embraces both demonic and apocalyptic or paradisal modes of elevated or epiphanic literature. There is, to use a fitting Blakean expression, a marriage of heaven and hell in Frye's notion of process literature, and this represents a radical departure from the move toward the terrible or Gothic sublime launched by Edmund Burke.

This gesture of inclusion in Frye reignites the essence of

Longinus's critical position wherein sublime literature is that literature which 'transports with wonder,' which 'exerts an irresistible force and mastery,' and which 'scatters everything before it like a thunderbolt,' revealing 'in a flash ... the full power of the speaker' (Longinus 100). There is here, as in Blake, the acknowledgment that imaginative power or mastery may engage a range of emotional modalities and that it is the *intensity* of the response that is primary. What is essential is the emotional transport in the experience of the reader, not necessarily the experience of fear, as Longinus's example of Sappho's 'A peer of the gods' ode underscores (Longinus 114). The implications of this inclusion of fear *and* pity, demonic *and* apocalyptic categories, within the critical class of 'process' represents the second principal aspect of Frye's Longinianism to be explored in this inquiry.

Although Longinus was concerned primarily with the rhetorical and poetic manifestation of sublimity, his preoccupation with elevation or transport necessarily implies a psychological component, and an interest in the relationship between language, thought, and emotion which was enthusiastically taken up in the late seventeenth and eighteenth centuries. Indeed, the central critical debates of this period on the question of the sublime may be seen to be contextualized within a broader set of questions concerning the nature of human understanding, and the operation of human taste and judgment. In the work of Edmund Burke, one of the many eighteenth-century thinkers who were to make the sublime the dominant aesthetic value of the age, this focus was given a decidedly materialistic bent. In Burke, in contrast to earlier treatments such as those of John Dennis, Robert Lowth, and Joseph Addison, the phenomenon of sublime experience was increasingly removed from the domain of rhetoric, poetry, and the mystico-religious, and applied instead to the realm of natural objects.[20] In his delineation of a 'natural sublime' and in his discussion of taste, Burke relied heavily on the inductive and empirical method which marked the earlier critical works of John Locke. Like Locke, Burke adopted a sensism that was not subjective (as was that of the earlier Hume and later Kant), but was rather primarily neuro-muscular and instinctual – one might be tempted to say, anachronistically, behaviouristic. Burke, like Frye, makes a clear distinction between art and the criticism of art saying, 'art can never give the rules that make an art' (Burke 54). Burke's treatise represents an attempt to inductively discriminate the rules or principles governing human aesthetic responses. It is an attempt to bring scientific rigour and objectivity to the realm of taste and to the operation of imagination, one of his three constitutive faculties of taste, the others being the senses and judgment: 'my point in this inquiry is to find whether there are any principles, on which the imagination is affected, so common to all, so grounded and certain, as to supply the means of reasoning satisfactorily about them. And such principles of taste, I fancy there are ...' (Burke 13).

Burke's essay on taste was in large part a polemical response to David Hume's *Dissertation on Taste*, which held that the norms of taste cannot be scientifically defined. Some years later, Blake, in turn, revolted against Burke's attempt at an objective and scientific, even a mechanistic, approach to taste and art, positing instead a radically subjective sublime resting on individual inspiration and vision. Instead of the senses, it is the imagination that takes the front seat in the roller-coaster ride of the sublime, and in this Blake follows on the heels of Giambattista Vico.

What is common to Vico, Blake, Burke, and Frye, and places them in sharp contrast to Immanuel Kant and the so-called educated sublime, is the portrayal of reason as incompatible with the sublime, and the concentration instead on the role of the 'primitive' mind-set in sublime or 'heightened' language. Frye, in noting that 'the primitive process of writing is projected in two directions, into nature and into history,' raises an issue which also preoccupied Vico for the better part of his life: namely, how, if sublimity is linked to the primitive, is it possible to experience and produce sublime poetry in a non-primitive age? Frye focuses on the 'psychologically primitive' as holding the key. In the literature of process, and especially in the poetry of process, what dominates is the oracular, autonomous, prophetic voice, often interpreted in the past to be the voice of the divine, while in more recent times frequently linked to that of insanity (*FI* 135–6). For Frye, as for

Vico, Blake, and Burke, the central feature of this 'primitive' ecstatic poetic mode is the radical, or as Frye calls it, the anagogic metaphor of identity: 'this is that' (136). Here, then, we may locate the third key element in Frye's formulation of process literature – one which finds its earliest articulation in the treatise of Longinus. In Vico, we, like Frye, may discern the first thinker to recognize the need to vindicate and preserve this mythopoeic mind-set, and the first to recognize its continuing underlying role in a world becoming increasingly secularized, scientifically rationalized, and, it would appear, demythologized (Costa, 'Considerazioni' 88).

Frye associates with process literature, particularly in the emotional register of 'pity without an object,' the 'sense of sympathy with man himself, the sense that no one can afford to be indifferent to the fate of anyone else.' He offers as examples the protests against slavery and misery in Cowper, in Crabbe, and in the *Songs of Experience* (*FI* 135). In opening a window onto the wider social implications of elevation in literature, Frye articulates a concern which was profoundly shared by Longinus, Vico, Blake, and the politically active Edmund Burke. If for no other reason, Frye's inclusion within the sphere of criticism of both Aristotelian and Longinian approaches is crucial in that it unequivocally establishes a place within the universe of literary criticism for considering the social and ethical ramifications of imaginative products. In process criticism as in process literature, a path is cleared for a critical consideration not just of the worlds constructed within the text, but also of how such creations impinge upon and shape the unfolding of the world.

two

Against a Separate Nature

I have proposed that after *Anatomy of Criticism,* Frye saw his critical task to be primarily (though not exclusively) the exploration of the process aspect of criticism rather than the objectifying and structuralist approach which he associated with the term 'product' and with the Aristotelian tradition. We are confronted, then, with the fact that his major works after *Anatomy,* namely, *The Great Code* and *Words with Power,* centre themselves on the Bible as the key text for critical examination. What was it that caused Frye to view the Bible as the appropriate text for exploring this zone of the critical terrain? In his introduction to *The Great Code,* Frye attempts to answer precisely this question; what he proposes is that the genuine critical issues of the day are 'closely related to the study of the Bible, and in fact are hampered by not being related more closely to it' (xviii).

As is usually the case with Frye, the roots of the question take us back to Blake, for it was Blake who taught Frye that 'the Bible had provided a mythological structure, which had expanded into a mythological universe, stretching from creation to apocalypse in time, from heaven to hell in space, and that this universe had formed a framework of imagery for all European poets down to his own time' (*SM* 108). Such a mythological universe is of necessity implicated in all human culture, and culture itself is described by Frye as the humanly constructed world that emerges out of human desire, as the 'total body of imaginative hypothesis in a society and its tradition' (*AC* 127). The biblical mythological universe is a key model of such a constructed or imaginative world. Blake seems to have awakened in Frye the intense conviction that this humanly created world of culture is a locus of power which may unleash a positive, transformative, and emancipating process in the world, effecting a form of rebirth or resurrection of humanity into a state of greater freedom, of reduced anxiety or concern (*SM* 115, 119).

As many critics have noted, this view of the transformative power of human imaginative products or worlds seems to implicate Frye in a nature versus culture dichotomy that may be seen as a valorization of culture, or in its originary sense, of myth, at the expense of a demonized natural order.[1] I will address this preliminary issue of the nature/culture dichotomy in Frye's thought before proceeding to examine, in a detailed way, Frye's theories of myth and metaphor as key aspects of his process approach to critical theory. As will emerge, Vico's own key critical and epistemological principles represent essential points of contact on all three questions and provide the unifying frame for the various aspects of Frye's Longinian approach to the verbal cultural domain.

No one has been more emphatic and dramatic in critiquing Frye's perceived ambivalence towards nature than has Daniel O'Hara who, in *The Romance of Interpretation: Visionary Criticism from Pater to de Man*, describes Frye as a Blakean visionary who, in the most systematic and schematic of ways, associates the natural with 'any and all blocking agents in the physical universe, in society, or in the writer's own psyche, that inhibit the quest for sublimity' (2). In *Fearful Symmetry*, Frye is seen by O'Hara to follow Blake in taking a nihilistic view of nature, associating it with a demonic and cyclical feminine drive which is contrasted to the liberating and redemptive function of art. O'Hara configures Frye's work ultimately as a 'defensive critical operation of self-discovery enacted against nature.' His conclusion: that Frye, the critic, is nothing if not *contra naturam* (204).

Although Frye does set out from a point of departure in his critical thinking that dichotomizes nature and culture, I do not conclude, as O'Hara does, that Frye's poetics (or, as O'Hara calls it, his 'aesthetics')[2] is, in the final analysis, 'anti-natural' (O'Hara

3). On the contrary, what I propose is that Frye's critical enterprise may be seen as unfolding into a quest for a reconciliation of
the natural and the cultural through the bridging work of the
imagination, and particularly, through the verbal or linguistic
products that it engenders.

At the personal level, Frye's ambivalence towards or discomfort
with the physical aspect of the natural world emerges very early.
John Ayre, Frye's biographer, quotes a letter addressed to his
wife Helen while he was studying at Oxford in 1936, in which he
wrote, '– if you ever get around to reading Lawrence's *Plumed
Serpent*, you will see how closely an exaggerated respect for nature
and her works is bound up with Fascism ...' (Ayre 127; *NFHK*
2:589). Earlier, during his student ministry in Saskatchewan, he
voiced his feeling of nature's aloofness, comparing it, ironically
enough, to the Bible, the text which was to be the focus of so
much of his scholarly endeavours: '"... the Bible is magnificent,
but, in spite of what everyone says, it is a book for admiration
rather than intimacy, like the natural world"' (Ayre 100; *NFHK*
1:243). This analogy is noteworthy for it implicitly recognizes the
contiguity of the human responses to nature and to the divine, a
contiguity rooted in feelings of awe and mystery which are, ultimately, at the heart of the sublime.

It was during this early period of abject mental and bodily
misery that Frye began his close study of Blake, and there is no
doubt that *Fearful Symmetry* represents an important first round in
Frye's attempt to clearly engage the issue of the relationship
between the human world of culture and the given order of the
natural. Like Blake, Frye conceived the world of culture as being
engaged in the radical transformation of the natural into the
embodied products of human creativity – a shaping and structuring of the alien, chaotic, and other into the recognizable, structured, and familiar; the transformation of a perceived inhospitable
objective order into the comfortable identity of an imaginatively
contrived home. This was based on 'Blake's idea of the image-
forming imagination which creates a paradisal garden out of the
wilderness of nature' (*FS* 170).

Speaking of the 'enthusiasm' experienced by the oracular or

prophetic poet who generates such a vision, Frye wrote: 'What then is this God-filled enthusiasm or fancy? Obviously the new rush of poetry about the solitary lover of nature meandering through rural surroundings with his head full of dreams does not represent a "return to nature" in any sense of a surrender to its influence. The fanciful poet is using nature as material, and is creating out of it a higher nature' (*FS* 170). O'Hara argues that this privileging of a 'second,' humanly constructed nature requires 'the sacrificial death of primary nature and so we can say that being for second nature always entails being against nature' (O'Hara 167).

There is no question that we may trace in Frye's thought considerable ambivalence towards the natural, physical order, even when we move beyond personal discomfiture and enter the realm of critical thinking and writing. He says in *The Educated Imagination* (1963), for example, 'underneath all the complexity of human life that uneasy stare at an alien nature is still haunting us, and the problem of surmounting it still with us' (22). In *Creation and Recreation*, a book to which we will turn again for its Vichian content, Frye wrote, 'Our envelope, as I have called it, the cultural insulation that separates us from nature, is ... [usually] a mirror of our own concerns, including our concern about nature. As a mirror, it fills us with the sense that the world is something which exists primarily in reference to us: it was created for us; we are the centre of it and the whole point of its existence' (*CR* 6; or, *NFR* 37–8). Here we see again that familiar image of the protective 'envelope' of culture (*CR* 5; or, *NFR* 37) which, like the maternal womb, protects humanity from a threatening, aloof, and mysterious environment, one which really is quite indifferent to humanity and, Frye suggests (in a tellingly bleak flight of fancy) would probably regret its complicity in the generation of humanity should it be capable of and interested in acknowledging it (*CR* 6; or, *NFR* 38).

Gerald Graff makes essentially the same observations as O'Hara, though in more temperate terms and with a more conservative ideological thrust, noting that Frye, like Kant, Hegel, Blake, and other romantic visionaries before him, assumes that humanity is somehow 'demeaned' if nature becomes the source of inspiration, and that the tyranny of nature can only be checked through the construction of a cultural home, that cultural 'envelope' or insulation of which Frye speaks repeatedly (*Literature Against Itself* 22). In the earlier *Poetic Statement and Critical Dogma*, Graff associated Frye with neo-Kantian thinkers such as Ernst Cassirer and Carl Jung who, in their philosophies of symbolic forms, proposed language as the locus of reality (65), and for whom nature is 'cold, dead, and unending' apart from man's imagination of it (65).

These critical reviews suggest just how pivotal and problematic is the polarization between nature and culture in Frye's thought. One of the most explicit statements of the nature/culture dichotomy may be found in the important essay 'Expanding Eyes' published in 1975:

> Man lives in two worlds, the world of nature which forms his external environment, and the constructed world of civilization and culture which he has made himself because he wants to live in such a world. The mythological universe is a model of the latter world ... It is a world built in the image of human desires and anxieties and preconceptions and ideals and objects of abhorrence, and it is always, and necessarily, geocentric and anthropocentric, which the actual environment is not. (*SM* 108–9)

The demonization of nature that O'Hara asserts underlies the 'curious dialectic of nihilism and idealism' in Frye's visionary work is tied to the feminine gendering of nature in the Western imagination, and this gendering is a crucial focus for Frye's exploration of the relationship between nature and culture. As O'Hara unambiguously states, Frye's association of the feminine principle with natural religion and the dead end implied thereby was clearly an inheritance from Blake and thus, inevitably, rooted in the Bible. We read in *Fearful Symmetry* the following on Blake and the feminine cast of nature:

> The material world is in a way feminine to the perceiver; it is the body which receives the seed of his imagination, and the works of the imagination which are the artist's children are drawn from that

body. We think of Nature as feminine, and so she is. But as the artist develops he becomes more and more interested in the art and more and more impatient of the help he receives from nature. In the world of Eden there is only energy incorporating itself in form, creator and creature, which means that somewhere ... this permanent objective body which nourishes and incubates the imaginative form drops out. Nature, in simple language, is Mother Nature, and in the perfectly imaginative state there is no mother. The fall of man began with the appearance of an independent object-world, and continued into this state of Generation, where we begin life in helpless dependence on Mother Nature for all our ideas. This independent nourishing force in nature Blake calls the female will. (*FS* 74–5)

Further along, Frye adds, 'Mother worship is womb-worship, a desire to prolong the helplessness of the perceiver and his dependence on the body of nature which surrounds him' (75). This is the imaginative paradigm that the Bible resists, for the Judaeo-Christian cosmology is not one which worships the divine in the form of the trinity of the father, mother, and child; rather, it is one of those 'more highly developed ones' where God is 'always the Supreme Male, the Creator for whom the distinction between the beloved female and created child has disappeared' (75).

O'Hara has drawn our attention to the maternal metaphors that dominate Frye's discussion of the feminine configuration of nature in the Western imagination. What he does not underscore sufficiently are the inferences to be drawn from the fact that the mother womb/tomb metaphor associated with nature and the contraints of nature's laws manages to find its way into the discussions of culture as well. In *Anatomy* Frye writes, 'the poet, who writes creatively rather than deliberately, is not the father of the poem; he is at best a midwife, or, more accurately still, the womb of Mother Nature herself: her privates he, so to speak'; and again, 'the poet has to give birth to the poem as it passes through his mind' (98). Here, however, the emphasis is on the liberation from the mother that comes with the process of birth or artistic production rather than on the latent gestation in the womb or the static terminal state of rest in the tomb. In this configuration, the poet gives birth to the creation, functioning as midwife, or, better still, as the conduit from inner to outer world. The poet has taken over the birthing function in all its multiplicity, becoming mother, midwife, and the very threshold where the process of cultural production unfolds. What Frye may be seen to be undertaking here is a destabilizing of the conventional application of the gender metaphors in the context of the nature/culture debates.

What is demonized both by Frye and Blake is not Nature *per se* but a 'separate nature' of 'elusive and treacherous beauty' that Frye, following Blake, describes as imaginatively pernicious, as coy and teasing (*FS* 74–5), a nature which is always calling but somehow remains out of reach, receding.

O'Hara argues that Frye's 'antithetical quest against Nature' and his 'complementary search for vision' represent an attempt to radically correct nature, through a degradation 'of nature, of history, of temporality, – in short of becoming' (177). Nature is projected by Frye, in O'Hara's analysis, as the 'Great Whore,' the demonic Blakean female will or Vala that must be 'stripped and burnt, so that the prophetic critic can produce from the ashes of this hermeneutic art the stark outlines of his ideal muse, who stands for his possible sublimity, his desired rebirth into symbolic immortality as a literary classic' (O'Hara 172). The figure of Vala as described by Frye in *Fearful Symmetry* is linked to a way of viewing nature as remote and alienated, in a word, as fallen, and it is through the processes of artistic creation that this objectifying and distancing perspective is undermined. Nature in the guise of female will is precisely 'the refusal of the beloved object to surrender this independence, which of course is really man's inability to make it do so'; it is the 'belief in an ultimate externality,' something that 'blocks our final vision,' our final identity (*FS* 263).

What becomes clear then, is that the feminine imaginative principle is associated with the objective body of matter, and this objectifying stance is what must be discarded in order to attain full imaginative potency of the 'highest' creative state, Eden – the realm not of the sexual, but of the creative act. It is the realm not of biological generation but of cultural production (*FS* 75). All female worship is disguised nature worship, and thus in terminology which we will encounter again in the context of the juxtapositioning of the beautiful and the sublime, Frye paraphrases Blake and condemns the imaginatively pernicious adoration of the mistress in Petrarchan and chivalric codes as a degenerate quest for the fallen, 'the elusive and treacherous beauty of a separate nature' (FS 75).

We should not find it surprising that this Blakean schema, in which the feminine is associated with an inferior aesthetic and epistemology, is in many ways echoed and prefigured in other eighteenth-century discourses on the sublime, and that it thus represents a daunting critical challenge for Frye. Terry Eagleton, in his recent detailed analysis of the sublime in *The Ideology of the Aesthetic*, discusses at some length Kant's association of the sublime with the masculine, and what is to be noted is the consistency of the attributes of the masculine sublime and the feminine beautiful in the Kantian and Burkean models with those traits that Frye isolates in his discussion of Blake's hierarchy of imaginative realms. Eagleton writes:

> The Kantian sublime is in effect a kind of unconscious process of infinite desire, which like the Freudian unconscious continually risks swamping and overloading the pitiable ego with an excess of affects. The subject of the sublime is accordingly decentred, and plunged into loss and pain, undergoes a crisis of and fading of identity; yet without this unwelcome violence we would never be stirred out of ourselves, never prodded into enterprise and achievement. We would lapse back instead into the placid feminine enclosure of the imaginary, where desire is captivated and suspended. Kant associates the sublime with the masculine and the military, useful antidotes against peace which breeds cowardice and effeminacy. (90)

Given the extent of Edmund Burke's influence on Kant,[3] it is not surprising to find that in Burke, too, the dialectic of the beautiful and sublime is configured metaphorically along gender lines.[4] In Burke, the sublime experience, a mixture of terror and delight, is privileged over the beautiful; it is associated with the pleasures of the mind, with 'the strongest emotions which the mind is capable of feeling' (39). The beautiful is, instead, associated with feelings, with love of the senses and physical pleasures of the body, but it is a love purged of all mystery, romance, and eroticism. The masculine sublime is linked to power, while the feminine beautiful is, at least ostensibly, tied to powerlessness. While the sublime objects are endowed by Burke and Kant with awe-inspiring, intellectually stimulating attributes which are tied to the cultivation of wisdom and justice, the beautiful are seen to be linked to less dignified qualities of the heart such as compassion and kindness (Burke 110). The sublime evokes a compulsion to withdraw, to place a safe distance between the feeling subject and the experienced object; the beautiful tempts one to approach, to touch. In keeping with the conventional, gender-based distribution of attributes, we see that the father-figure is proffered as an example of the object that inspires the sublime response, while the mother is held up as being associated with the beautiful. Other attributes follow the paradigm in like measure: large versus small; angular and rectilinear versus rounded and flowing; strong versus weak; infinite versus temporal; and so on.

The dynamics at work here go beyond sexual stereotypes and a possible sublimation of homophilia; what we are presented with is the discourse of power. Burke explicitly describes the experience of the sublime as one of being dominated or captured by a superior power, and the description verges on that of a rapturous rape of the self. In contrast, the relationship between the subject and object in the case of the beautiful is occasionally described as a possession of the object by the subject, but it is also explicitly depicted as a seduction of the subject by the object. There is little discussion of rapture or pleasure in this seduction, however, but rather hostility, suspicion, and, ironically, fear. Burke juxtaposes a masculine overpowering through sheer unmitigated force in the operation of the sublime, against a stereotypical feminine seduction through flattery, scheming, and subterfuge in the case of the beautiful (113). What emerges as significant is not, therefore, the exercise of power by an object over a subject, but rather the manner in which this process unfolds. In language heavily loaded with the paranoia of misogyny, Burke describes a beautiful woman, focusing exclusively on her neck and breasts, on the 'deceitful maze, through which the unsteady eye slides giddily, without knowing where to fix, or whither it is carried' (115). Burke also alludes to the female's strategic cultivation of imperfection and of the appearance of weakness as part of the agenda of surreptitious seduction (110). It is to be noted that Burke, unlike Longinus, relegates the concealed exercise or manipulation of aesthetic attraction, not to the realm of the sublime, but to that of the beautiful. What Burke presents us with is *not* a model in which the sublime represents power and the beautiful subjugation, but rather one in which the seduction effected by the beautiful is, ultimately, more terrible than the delight provoked by the sublime. This subtext is paradoxically camouflaged by a superficial domestication of love of the beautiful as a 'mere positive pleasure' (160).

In spite of the many important shadings of difference that may be discerned in the respective discourses on the sublime and the beautiful of Burke, Kant, and Blake, what we note consistently is a tendency to privilege the sublime for its association with mind, human subjectivity, and the masculine, while the beautiful is consistently and with considerable underlying anxiety linked to the body, the objective physical order, and the feminine. Notwithstanding the powerful impact that eighteenth-century gendering of the key aesthetic categories of the sublime and the beautiful may initially have had on Frye (as we may note particularly in *Fearful Symmetry*), we may detect in his work over time an attempt to mitigate and correct the misapprehensions that such structuring metaphors, with their biblical roots, have nurtured.

In Frye's more recent publications there is present a concerted attempt to reorient the import of these gender metaphors and the epistemological baggage they have come to assume. What these efforts represent is work aimed at salvaging the visionary stance while moving in step with an epoch increasingly embracing Gaia. In *Creation and Recreation*, Frye acknowledges the regrettable exploitation of the biblical creation myths and their use of gender symbols to promote a patriarchal social ideology, and goes on to note that, 'It would be useful if Western thought had developed something like the classical Chinese conception of *yang* and *yin,* which would express something of the imaginative and mythological relations of male and female without perverting them' (*CR* 37; or, *NFR* 58). David Cayley, in *Northrop Frye in Conversation*, asked Frye whether or not he had been thinking about the fact that in the present age of concern with ecology, an 'immanentalist, Buddhist type of philosophy' is more attractive than the Judaeo-Christian because it does not objectify creation and separate humanity from it to the same extent (205). Frye's answer was to elucidate the biblical position while accepting that it has had problematic results:

> I think that the way the Bible deals with this question is confusing to most readers, because we've got two bodies of imagery to deal with. One is humanity versus physical environment. The other is the sexual image of man and woman. The fall was, as I say, a pollution of sex. Adam and Eve knew that they were naked and started to make clothes. Therefore, rehabilitation – going the opposite way from the fall – would be, among other things, a rehabilitation of sex. So that the relation of man and nature would become part of the relation of love ... It's explicitly said that the patriarchal society is a result of sin, a result of the fall. So that to go the other way would be to restore the original love relationship between humanity and physical nature. (205)

Frye goes on to caution that this relationship between humanity and nature is one of creature to creature; the sacred is not in nature though 'you may use images from nature in expressing sacredness' (*NFC* 206). The relationship to be rehabilitated between the human and the rest of the natural order is, it would appear, some kind of intersubjective one, one that Frye has, as noted, described as 'interpenetrative.' As he has repeatedly observed in his later writing, this rehabilitation of the relationship between humanity and nature seems to go hand in hand with the rehabilitation of man's relationship with woman.[5]

Frye recognized that Blake's gendered theory of imagination

was problematic. The imaginative stance associated with the feminine, Beulah, is ultimately a perilous one, one that teeters on the verge of a collapse into the completely vegetative state of Generation or Ulro (*FS* 233–4). Beulah, like the profile of beauty in Kant and Burke, is an imaginative mode that is centred in the body and is associated with passivity, laconic pleasure, and indolence (*FS* 233). It is a state of imminent fall or collapse into nature and the inevitable cycle of birth, death, and rebirth.

Frye went back to confront this problematic area in Blake's thought in the essay 'Blake's Bible' and conceded there that 'some personal anxieties may also have obscured the clarity of this part of his vision' and may account for Blake's surprising lack of interest in the Song of Songs (*MM* 282–3) and for his tendency to view the creation of Eve as the real fall. Blake takes up, in *The Four Zoas*, the Bible's suggestion that in the second creation account of Genesis, the Jahwist, what is depicted is an androgynous Adam surrounded by a symbolically female garden; furthermore, over and over we note in Blake the paradigm of a symbolically male humanity existing within the clutches of a symbolically female nature representing a demonic or fallen world. Frye suggests that the counter-balance for this negative symbolism associating the feminine with an objectified and remote natural order may be discerned in the daughters or 'emanations' of Albion in *Jerusalem*, who represent the totality of what Albion constructs, loves, and surrounds himself with, in a clear evocation of the paradisal vision that concludes the Book of Job. It is a vision of man united with a nature that is now in his image, created by him and thus contained in him, rather than representing his physical entrapment and limitations. But even such attempts at rehabilitation cannot mitigate the fact that in Blake's mythological and symbolic structures, the cost of a visionary cosmology is the symbolic exclusion of nature as nature.

Frye had to move beyond Blake's gender-imaged cosmology in order to satisfy himself on this point. The first step in this direction was taken in the early paper on eighteenth-century sensibility, which expresses in a most explicit way the core of his notion of process in poetics. Frye's discrimination of the overarching critical categories of 'product' and 'process' has, in effect, removed the objectification stance previously associated metaphorically with a feminine and alienated natural or 'fallen' order and with the Burkean notion of 'beauty,' and purged such categories of their gender associations, rendering them, as it were, neutral. Frye's notion of process literature traces a Longinian poetics, which accommodates a broad range of emotional and figurative modalities but rests on a distinct ontology and epistemology which is equally receptive to masculine and feminine metaphorical paradigms, to apocalytic and demonic symbolic structures. It is a poetic and aesthetic category from which much ideological debris of a bygone era has been, at last, cleared away. In the intense, emotively charged experience of literature (and by implication, of the world) as process, both fear and pity, awe and sympathy, may be emotional vehicles for a heightened, non-objectifying state of being.

For Frye the experience of process is not defined by the category of emotion experienced, nor is it figured through the insidious use of the conventional gendered metaphors; rather, it is associated first and foremost with an intense identification of the subject with an emotionally enlivened, non-objectified world. Whatever the focus may be, the ontological stance is a radically intersubjective one and the epistemology implicit in it is founded on a model of knowledge which, as Vico helped Frye to understand, is rooted in the harnessing of metaphor's relational powers. It is not coincidental that Frye concludes this important essay with a discussion of metaphor and psychologically primitive and oracular poetry. In the prophetic, quasi-ecstatic processes of radical or anagogic metaphor, there is, he states, a 'white-hot fusion of identity' between nature and the poet in which the reader may, if so inclined, also participate (FI 137). This fusion or identity that metaphor structures is the key to Frye's notion of process, and it is the experiential place where nature and culture make contact. Frye's great revisionary critical project is not, as O'Hara and Graff have proposed, to supercede nature, but rather to show how, in the world of culture, there is a reconciling of the humanly natural, that is, of creative, imaginative activities, with the non-human natural world. Frye describes this lively process as 'interpenetration' in a pointed use of non-gendered sexual imagery which is pivotal in Frye's theoretical formulations and which will be discussed in greater detail below.

I have shown, then, how Frye succeeded in neutralizing the excessive and ideologically insidious use of gendering metaphors that is noticeable in Blakean, Burkean, and Kantian discourses on the beautiful and sublime by incorporating ungendered discussions of these aesthetic categories within the meta-category of 'process.' The underlying preoccupation here is the question of humanity's ability to be reconciled to nature via the mythopoeic processes that are intrinsic to culture. This is made more manifest in Frye's later writings, where the dichotomy of product versus process, the objectification of the world versus intersubjective identification with it, is linked in a direct way to the unfolding of distinct modalities of *langage* over the course of human cultural history. Before we turn to the examination of Frye's theories of myth and metaphor and their place in process criticism, our attention will be directed to the common Longinian tradition shared by Vico and Frye, and to a close examination of those aspects of Vico's thought that approach, in a significant way, Frye's poetics of process.

three

Vico and the Making of Truth

The key question that fuelled Giambattista Vico's monumental and influential elaboration of his 'new science' of humanity was one centrally linked to the nature/culture dichotomy; namely, How are we to understand the transition of humanity from a state of nature to a state of culture or civilization? What is implicated in Vico's response is a notion which Frye has termed 'creative alienation' and which may be seen to encompass the prototypical paradigm of the sublime experience – the experience of awe, terror, and subsequent empowerment that arises from an intense awareness of the being of the world and an elevated consciousness of self in that world. That Frye, like Vico and Burke, understands the confrontation with the other that is paradigmatic of the sublime to be a critical impetus for the unfolding of culture is clear:

> One can see the importance, for poets and others, of the remoteness and otherness of nature: the feeling that the eighteenth century expressed in the word 'sublime' conveys to us that there is such a thing as creative alienation. The principle laid down by the Italian philosopher Vico of *verum factum*, that we understand only what we have made ourselves, needs to be refreshed sometimes by the contemplation of something we did not make and do not understand. (*CR* 5–6; or, *NFR* 37)

In 'Frye, Vico, and the Grounding of Literature and Criticism,' Domenico Pietropaolo has argued that Frye's critical theory 'may be fruitfully interpreted as being itself grounded in Vico' ('*Ritratto di Northrop Frye* 88). He also points out that 'Vico's lifelong quest for the science of man's coming to humanity ... is exactly analogous to Frye's pursuit of the science of literature,' (89) and that both sciences are founded on a recognition of mythology's grounding function in human culture and literature. Pietropaolo continues his line of argument by suggesting that

> Frye, as a literary critic, turns to the philosophy of the originative character of poetic thinking, presupposed by mythology, only for the light that it can shed on the phenomenological status of the literary work, whose structure has been the principle focus of his long career, while Vico, as a philosopher seeking to uncover the principles – chronological, epistemological, and ontological – of man's rise to humanity, holds his gaze fixed on the mythological structure in order to grasp the civilizing impulse of the poetic thinking that grounds it, rather than to disclose the structural patterns of the literary works that are grounded in it. (89)

These observations, though very apt with respect to Frye's early work, must be qualified in view of Frye's later scholarly engagements. Here two distinct critical impulses must be seen to emerge: the structuralist or Aristotelian approach that has been identified with the term 'product,' and the Longinian critical slant with which his concept of 'process' has been linked.[1] What I am stating here, in a very explicit way, is that with respect to this second, process-based aspect of Frye's critical task, his concerns parallel in a very proximate sense those of Giambattista Vico; indeed, to the extent that Frye is prepared to engage the theological aspects of the poetic endeavour, he may be seen to push the Vichian agenda into realms which his 'guide,' like Virgil, could not access.[2]

Gustavo Costa, a long-time commentator on both Giambattista Vico and the Longinian tradition, has recognized that Vico and Frye form part of a Romantic critical tradition rooted in Longinus's treatise *On the Sublime*.[3] With respect to Vico, he writes that 'Perhaps Vico was the first to intuit how much was happening in the final period of transition from the prescientific to the scientific mentality, if one considers his vindication of the mythical and magical dimension, one not to be distinguished from sublime poetry' ('Considerazione inattuali sul sublime' 86) [This and subsequent translations from the Italian are mine].[4] Arguing for a tradition and perspective on the sublime which extends beyond the 'purely rhetorical' (89), Costa notes the linking of Longinus's treatise with the numinous in the Bible, a text to which the treatise makes several noteworthy references in its search for examples of poetic sublimity (90). The connection between the aesthetic of the sublime and mystico-religious experience is one that Costa carefully acknowledges as he surveys the many associations of ecstatic poetry with the prophetic function (90–1). This prophetic strain in poetics is one that is incontrovertibly a concern for Frye, as Costa himself observes:

> The West became Romantic, recognizing itself in the idea of the creative imagination, which bestows on the artist a power analogous to that of God, who created the world *ex nihilo*. This creation, one quite removed from the Greek spirit, could be more easily reconciled with the vague mysticism of Pseudo-Longinus than with Aristotle, and so Occidental criticism became Longinian. Even today the critical task is practised between the poles staked out by Aristotle and Pseudo-Longinus, if Northrop Frye was able to adopt a conception of literature of a thematic and creative Longinian cast, founded on the ecstatic in contrast to an aesthetic and detached Aristotelian conception of literature founded on catharsis.[5]

The close links between Frye's *theoria* of criticism and his theological concerns shall be more thoroughly explored in due course. I note here, however, that the word 'process,' which Frye has adopted to describe what is essentially the Longinian tradition in criticism, is a term centrally implicated in a theological movement known as 'process theology.' This movement blossomed in the 1960s and 1970s, and is rooted in the philosophical work of Alfred North Whitehead, particularly in his *Process and Reality*.[6] References to Whitehead in Frye's published works are rather sparse, but it should be noted that such important references do emerge in the two volumes on the Bible and in an essay first published in 1983 entitled 'Literature as a Critique of Pure Reason' (included in the important collection of essays entitled *Myth and Metaphor*, 1990). These references usually arise in the context of important discussions of metaphor and imagination (*MM* 169, 171; *GC* 17; *WP* 12, 150).[7] As our exploration of Frye's meditations on anagogic metaphor and *kerygma* will eventually detail, there is substantial and noteworthy overlap between the essential aspects of process theology and process criticism, and this overlap is rooted in a parallel epistemology the fundamental outlines of which were traced by Giambattista Vico. Not surprisingly, we find in Frye's unpublished private writings a reference to Vico which explicitly connects him to the 'process-philosophies': 'The fact that birth implies death suggests an endlessly turning wheel. Telos is incarnation or embodiment in reverse, the wheel of chronos reaching a point of *kairos*. With Vico the maya wheel reappears in the West, & since then we have developed mayan process-philosophies, which tend to deprive the intellect of a focus' (NB 19, par. 150).

Vico restricted his inquiry into 'the course that nations run' to gentile history, while explicitly bracketing Hebrew history and the biblical narrative. This is certainly understandable given the lively activities of the Inquisition in the Naples of his day. His reticence may also be ascribed to the fact that Vico never did resolve in a satisfactory way the tension between 'his faith and his humanistic historicism, between his conception of the cunning of Providence, and his constant emphasis on the creative and self-transforming labours of men' (Berlin, *Vico and Herder* 82).[8] This is an accommodation that Frye, with the help of William Blake, was able to achieve. But Vico's epistemology represents an invaluable guidepost for tracing the path that this accommodation takes in laying the groundwork for a process criticism founded on process philosophy and embracing a type of process theology as well.

What are the Vichian elements in Frye's thought, then, that link him to this 'process' tradition in Western critical thinking and allow him to substantially build on it? The answer must incorporate in a major way what Domenico Pietropaolo has referred to as the grounding function of mythopoeic thinking and the radically metaphorical nature of such thought ('Frye, Vico' 94). It also must take into account the profoundly humanistic epistemological tenets of Vico's *verum factum* principle which Frye, with the added impetus of Blake, has made his own.

One of the most extensive recent studies of Vico's theory of knowledge is contained in Isaiah Berlin's *Vico and Herder: Two Studies in the History of Ideas* of 1976.[9] The crucial point that Berlin makes here is that among Vico's great innovations was the denial of a fixed *a priori* human nature, and the postulating instead of a model of humanity awash in the flux of a self-making process driven by collective human needs (37–9). For Vico, then, the key to fully human status must be sought 'within the modifications of the mind of him who mediates it. For since this world of nations has certainly been made by men, it is within these modifications that its principles should have been sought' (*NS* 374). Operative here, apart from the Renaissance belief in human self-transcendence, are scholastic meditations on the divine creative *logos* which was analogized into a human context. What was effected in the process was the redressing of those imbalances that arose from Descartes's misplaced confidence in the logical, deductive method and the Lockean notion of *tabula rasa* induction.[10]

Preliminary formulations of the *verum factum* axiom may be found in Vico's early writings. Although these minor works, which arose in the form of inaugural addresses, will be much more fully explored in due course, I want to glance briefly at them here in the context of the eighteenth-century discourse on the sublime. Gustavo Costa has argued in his article 'Vico and Ancient Rhetoric' that in the early writings, such as the oration entitled *On the Most Ancient Wisdom of the Italians* of 1710, we may discern the strong influence of Longinus's treatise and of the related Franco-Italian debates in fostering Vico's anti-rationalist tendencies (254). In another oration of the previous year entitled *On the Study Methods of Our Time* Vico again adopts an anti-rationalist stance, setting up a clear dichotomy between sublimity of thought and style on the one hand, and abstract, analytical reasoning on the other. He also proceeds to identify the latter primarily with French language in much the same manner as does Edmund Burke in his important inquiry into aesthetic taste, and particularly in the context of his commentary on the beautiful and the sublime.

Like Vico, Burke implicitly adopts an anti-Cartesian and anti-scholastic stance which concludes in finding French language and logic to be inconsistent with sublimity of thought and style:

> It may be observed that very polished languages, and such as are praised for their superior clearness and perspicuity, are generally deficient in strength. The French language has that perfection, and that defect. Whereas the Oriental tongues, and in general the languages of most unpolished people, have a great force and energy of expression; and this is but natural. (176)

In this juxtapositioning of reason or critical judgment and imagination, both Vico and Burke are influenced, no doubt, by Longinus's contrast between precision on the one hand and the marvellous on the other.[11] A close scrutiny of Burke's position reveals that it is premised on a Vichian understanding of the fundamental link between the primitive and the imaginative:

> Uncultivated people are but ordinary observers of things, and not critical in distinguishing them, but for that reason, they admire more and are themselves more affected with what they see, and therefore express themselves in a warmer and more passionate manner. (176)

Gustavo Costa actually suggests the possibility that, in view of the fact that the oration *On the Study Methods* was published in England in 1710, while Burke's *Enquiry* first appeared in 1757, Burke was directly influenced by Vico's thought.[12] It is thus not surprising to find that in Burke, as in Vico, we may locate an emphatic and explicit description of the sublime as entailing a discontinuity between the emotions and the imagination on the one hand and reason on the other:

> the mind is so entirely filled with its [great or sublime] object, that it cannot entertain any other, nor by consequence reason on that

object which employs it. Hence arises the great power of the sublime, that far from being produced by them, it anticipates our
reasonings, and hurries us on by an irresistible force. (57)

Reason or the critical judgment has been left behind in Burke's
sublime moment and only the senses and the imagination (which
included, for Burke, the emotions) are left in play. This divorcing
of reason and imagination becomes crucial in the context of
Burke's poetic or literary sublime and represents a significant
point of contact with both Vico and Frye.

Although it is primarily in his investigation of the poetic sublime that Burke's privileging of imagination and emotion over
reason is elaborated, this point is also underscored in the introductory essay on taste and in those parts of the *Enquiry* devoted
to the so-called natural sublime: 'the judgement is for the greater
part employed in throwing stumbling blocks in the way of the
imagination, in dissipating scenes of its enchantment: and in
tying us down to the disagreeable yoke of reason' (Burke 25). It
is this attitude towards the faculties of abstract reasoning that has
earned Burke the reputation of being 'anti-intellectual' and that
leads to contrasts with the 'educated' sublime of Wordsworth
and Kant.[13]

As Joseph Mali has discussed in *The Rehabilitation of Myth: Vico's
New Science* (1992), Vico linked the original poetic genius of early
humanity to the sublimity of the primitive mind. What this creative process entailed was actually the sublimation of emotions by
means of the displacement that art or poetry afforded (194).
According to Vico, early man was a poet effortlessly and unconsciously, acting out of a necessity born of ignorance, for 'when
man understands he extends his mind and takes in the things but
when he does not understand he makes the things out of himself
and becomes them by transforming himself into them' (*NS* 405).
For Vico sublimity is directly related to the human state of civilization, for the term 'sublime' implies precisely the ability of man to
liberate himself by means of human speech from his submersion
in nature: 'these theological poets, unable to make use of the
understanding, did the opposite and more sublime thing: they

attributed senses and passions ... to bodies as vast as sky, sea, and earth' (*NS* 402). Language and thought are seen to emerge in humanity by means of a 'wholly corporeal imagination' (*NS* 376) that feeds on emotionally particularized experiences which are isolated from the chaotic flux of sensory reception, impressed on consciousness and stored in the memory in the form of anthropomorphic similitudes. These similitudes or, more accurately, metaphors, are founded *not* on resemblance but on identification (*NS* 363).[14] Like Burke, Vico took as his point of departure for imaginative functioning the ground of the bodily senses and, as his poetic reconstruction of the first such revolutionary reaction illustrates, the model also conforms to Burke's prototype of the 'terrible sublime,' as a still beast-like man is shocked and terrified by a post-diluvial storm into contriving a thundering sky-father (*NS* 377). Vico explicitly describes originary human creativity as entailing the generation of sublime poetry through the medium of this body-based imagination:

In such fashion the first men of the gentile nations, children of nascent mankind, created things according to their own ideas. But this creation was infinitely different from that of God. For God, in his purest intelligence, knows things, and, by knowing them creates them; but they, in their robust ignorance, did it by virtue of a wholly corporeal imagination. And because it was quite corporeal, they did it with marvellous sublimity; a sublimity such and so great that it excessively perturbed the very persons who by imagining did the creating, for which they were called 'poets,' which is the Greek for 'creators.' (*NS* 376)

As Gustavo Costa has suggested in his essay 'G.B. Vico e lo pseudo-Longino,' it is fitting that Vico should situate *the* archetypal and primordial sublime experience on a mountain, and also that Vico, who was carefully circumscribing a safe intellectual space in a dangerous time, should nevertheless have implicitly underscored the fundamental connection between religion and sublime poetic activity (525). Vico proceeds from his discussion of poetic creativity and the description of 'the threefold labour of great poetry' (namely, the invention of sublime fables, excessive perturbation, and the teaching of virtue to the vulgar [*NS* 376]) to a re-enactment of the earliest such experiences of the sublime:

> Of such natures must have been the first founders of gentile humanity when ... at last the sky fearfully rolled with thunder and flashed with lightning, as could not but follow from the bursting upon the air for the first time of an impression so violent. Thereupon a few giants, who were dispersed through the forests on the mountain heights where the strongest beasts have their dens, were frightened and astonished by the great effect whose cause they did not know, and raised their eyes and became aware of the sky. And because in such a case the nature of the human mind leads it to attribute its own nature to the effect, and because in that state their nature was that of men all robust bodily strength, who expressed their very violent passions by shouting and grumbling, they pictured the sky to themselves as a great animated body, which in that aspect they called Jove, the first god of the so-called greater gentes, who meant to tell them something by the hiss of his bolts and the clap of his thunder. (*NS* 377)

For Vico the sublimity of poetry arises not from a refinement of ideas and sensibilities but through the intensity of body-based sensation and emotion displaced or sublimated into anthropomorphic projections of nature. Although Vico and Frye adhere to a privileging of the primitive in the mythopoeic, their positions are rendered even more proximate by their insistence, as educators, on the fact that such an attitude or frame of mind may, indeed must, be cultivated through education and kept alive as a saving remnant through all the turns that human cultural history takes. Longinus maintained, with Horace and other early critics, that sublimity is an inborn gift, a nobility of soul or character, that must, however, be nurtured in order to be put to proper use:

> Genius, they say, is innate; it is not something that can be learnt, and nature is the only art that begets it ... Nature is the first cause and fundamental creative principle in all activities, but the function of a

system is to prescribe the degree and the right moment for each, and to lay down the clearest rules for use and practice. Furthermore, sublime impulses are exposed to greater dangers when they are left to themselves without ballast and stability of knowledge; they need the curb as often as the spur. (Longinus, ch. 2)

Where Vico surpassed Longinus and other classical theorists was in his insistence, in opposition to Plato, that poetry, not philosophy, founded gentile humanity (*NS* 214). Through the concrete and particular schemata of metaphor and their narrative extensions in myth, humanity imagined/created its first experience of reality – one different from, but essentially a precursor to, abstractive and rational thought. Instead of positing a dichotomized view, like Plato's, in which poetry and philosophy are juxtaposed, Vico attempted to trace their complementarity and explore the ways in which they are associated. As we shall see, Frye's important first chapter in *The Great Code* represents an elaboration on this very aspect of Vico's critical undertaking. But before examining Frye's Vichian project, let us acquaint ourselves with the essential parameters of Vico's thought, particularly with those three aspects that most closely touch on Frye's concerns: myth, metaphor, and the *verum factum* principle.

In his early writings, Vico laid the foundation for an anti-rationalist and anti-Cartesian epistemology and pedagogy which inform all central aspects of the *New Science*. Vico's anti-rationalism sprang from the recognition that the premises of Descartes were, like the 'givens' of algebra, bound to ensure a tautological nicety of argument that falls far short of imaginative or metaphorical thinking in terms of cognitive and speculative fecundity. The fundamental methodological principles for Vico became the insistent questioning and dismantling of long-entrenched conceptual premises and ideological biases, as well as the radical refusal to accept the view that language and its 'surface' structures are devoid of speculative significance. As will be demonstrated, it is by working with these very surface structures of language, namely, through etymology and philology, and through the rhetorical and tropological investigation of figures, tropes, and particularly, metaphor, that Vico extracts his most profound insights regarding language, thought, and distinctively human being. Vico's work represents not only a dialectic advocating the epistemological and pedagogical rewards to be reaped from the study of philology and rhetoric; it is also the *exemplum* or demonstration of the cognitive rewards such approaches, which we would today call 'deconstructive,' may yield.

It is in the inaugural oration of 1709, *De nostri temporis studiorum ratione* (*On the Study Methods of Our Time*, henceforth *Study Methods*), that Vico first engages in a polemical encounter with Descartes, setting out, point by point, an essentially humanist alternative to the logico-deductive method and epistemology outlined in the *Discours de la méthode*. This oration not only contains, in nucleus, the complex insights into language and thought which would be elaborated in painstaking detail in *The New Science*; it also displays the focus on figures of speech and the philological techniques which allowed Vico to reach the seminal conclusions of *The New Science*. With this oration, Vico entered the fray of the *querelle*, arguing, with a vengeance, the necessity of maintaining at the heart of education and speculation, even in the face of the 'new method' of Descartes, the 'practical wisdom of the ancients':

> In conclusion: whosoever intends to devote his efforts, not to physics or mechanics, but to a political career, whether as a civil servant or as a member of the legal profession or of the judiciary, a political speaker or a pulpit orator, should not waste too much time, in his adolescence, on those subjects which are taught by abstract geometry. Let him, instead, cultivate his mind with an ingenious method; let him study topics, and defend both sides of the controversy, be it on nature, man, or politics, in a freer and brighter style of expression. Let him not spurn reasons that wear a semblance of probability and verisimilitude. Let our efforts not be directed towards achieving superiority over the Ancients merely in the field of science, while they surpass us in wisdom; let us not be merely more exact and more true than the Ancients, while allowing them to be more eloquent than we are; let us equal the Ancients in the fields of wisdom and eloquence as we excel them in the domain of science.[15]

As this passage makes clear, *Study Methods* is characterized by the juxtaposition of topics to criticism, of inventive or imaginative thinking to analytical or deductive thought, and what the privileging of topics and invention reflects is not merely a pedagogical bias, but a nascent metaphysics emerging from the distinction between the true or certain and the probable or verisimilar.[16]

For Descartes and the rationalists, imagination, with its reliance on a sensory experience grounded in the corporeal, indicates intellectual weakness, a contamination of the pure, the abstract, and the universal with the gross, the concrete, and the particular. In contrast to this, Vico utilizes practical psychological insights gleaned from that keen observation of human behaviour which lies at the heart of rhetorical pragmatics. Figuration and the repetition of imagery, rather than impeding thought, appears to be of great advantage in accessing and retaining concepts; furthermore, a stronger impact will be made on a listener (or reader) by avoiding the bald statement of truths or principles, and constructing instead a verbal edifice by means of which the listener (or reader) is brought to achieve the desired conclusion through her own mental gymnastics (*Opere* 185; Gianturco trans. 25). In what is *the* crucial passage of this oration, Vico advances his discourse from the realm of performative pragmatics to a subversive insistence on the link between philosophical or speculative activity and metaphor:

All the modern physicists affect a style of exposition which is as severe as it is limited. Our theory of physics (in the process of learning as well as when mastered) moves forward by a constant and gradual series of small, closely catenated steps. Consequently, it is apt to smother the student's specifically philosophical faculty, i.e. his capacity to perceive the analogies existing between matters lying far apart and, apparently, most dissimilar. It is this capacity which constitutes the source and principle of all ingenious, acute, and brilliant forms of expression. It should be emphasized that tenuity, subtlety, delicacy of thought, is not identical with acuity of ideas. That which is tenuous, delicately refined, may be represented by a single line; 'acute' by two. Metaphor, the greatest and brightest

ornament of forceful, distinguished speech, undoubtedly plays the
first role in acute, figurative expression. (Gianturco trans., 24)[17]

Here Vico utilizes a technique which is fundamental to his
method and which serves to reinforce his theories; namely, the
dismantling of long-established figures of speech in order to expose
and recuperate their original visual and conceptual impact. The
rote and, by Vico's time, perfunctory baroque definition of metaphor as 'an acute and ornate saying' is unpackaged here when Vico
releases the significance congealed in its deadened metaphorical
frame. Vico accomplishes this by elaborating on the geometric and
visual differences inherent between the *sottile* (visualized as a fine
line or ray) and the *acuto* (the sharp or acute angle). Vico was to
make much more of this geometric imagery in subsequent texts,
and its conceptual adroitness and importance should not be un-
derestimated. In the composition of an acute angle two lines must
be brought into contact at a common point or place. The analogy
to the invention of a third term or *quid medium* in topics is intentional and implicit, for what is involved in metaphor is the passage
from the 'proper' or literal sense of an expression to its figurative
one through the contriving of a common third term. This common
point or link represents a dialectical synthesis, the construal of a
sense from the dissonance of the metaphorical is and is not.

In this passage, Vico's anti-Cartesianism merges with anti-
scholasticism and anti-French sentiment as he polemically contrasts Italian *ingegno* (inventive wit) with French *esprit* (analytical
or critical judgment), arguing that while the former is occupied
with the 'composition of unities of thought,' the latter is engaged
only in refining them. Given the proclivities of the French language, Vico argues, only the French could have devised the new
criticism (the Cartesian method) consisting entirely, as it does, of
esprit; and only the French could have invented the new analytical
method which had all but divested the mathematical sciences of
corporeity. Accordingly, the only eloquence which the French
appear to savour is one consisting of logically true and subtle
pronouncements, arranged with ordered, deductive rigour (*Opere*
200; Gianturco trans. 40).

For our purposes, the polarity between the body-centredness of inventive wit or *ingenium* and the 'spirituality' or abstraction of analytical or deductive reasoning is of particular concern; however, we should also note that Vico is suggesting that the morphological and syntactical as well as the semantic aspects of the various languages reflect and perhaps influence the thought processes of their respective speakers. In support of this he points out that the large number of nouns and the short period which typify the French language are consistent with a predilection for abstraction rather than invention or induction (*Opere* 199; Gianturco trans. 39–40). Although Vico has clearly overstated the case by conflating rationalism with French language and thought, the correlation between modalities of verbal expression and types of mental or intellective functions that is emerging here will prove pivotal in Vico's subsequent work.

It is the inventive aspect of figurative language that Vico is extolling in *Study Methods*, and we may discern from this the fact that Vico has already turned away from a notion of truth based on certainty as he begins to posit instead a truth founded on human creativity. In a passage which clearly privileges the ideality of poetic truth, Vico underscores the internal contradictions inherent in a notion of truth based on the factual certainty of a reality chiefly characterized by imperfection:

> Practical judgment in human affairs seeks out the truth as it is, although truth may be deeply hidden under imprudence, ignorance, whim, fatality, or chance; whereas poetry focuses her gaze on truth as it ought to be by nature and reason. (Gianturco trans. 43)[18]

Shaking long-established ideological premises inside-out, Vico begins to formulate his radically innovative notion of truth as being ideal and invented – in short, poetic: 'He [the poet] departs from inconstant, unpredictable nature in order to pursue a more constant, more abiding reality. He creates imaginary figments which, in a way, are more real than physical reality itself' (Gianturco trans. 43).[19] What is noteworthy here is Vico's ability to tease sense from paradox; it is that transgressive talent for breaking down the linear compartmentalization of logic in order to conjure up a novel and meaningful configuration on the very back of the logical obstruction. In making the apparent contradiction 'false is true' meaningful, Vico has with sublime ease encapsulated and illustrated the essence of the long and arduous intellectual journey that lay before him.

The second critical juncture in Vico's reflections on language and thought emerges in his first major publication, *De antiquissima Italorum sapientia* (*On the Most Ancient Wisdom of the Italians*, henceforth *Ancient Wisdom*),[20] published in 1710. This text, modelled on Plato's *Cratylus*, adopts as its primary approach the etymological and philological investigation of crucial Latin words, ostensibly in order to reconstruct the mode of thinking of the early Italian philosophers. What emerges, however, is a reaffirmation, elaboration and fortification of those polemical propositions which first began to coalesce in *Study Methods*. Moreover, it is apparent in this second text that, out of his participation in the Franco-Italian debate over truth and inventive wit, Vico was beginning to fashion a theory of cognition and, specifically, of the genesis of cognition.

Vico wastes little time in *Ancient Wisdom* before attacking the tautological and ironically illogical nature of Descartes's *cogito*. This ill-founded principle emerges, Vico insists, from a resigned ignorance regarding the roots of human thinking, and from a tendency to forget that man is body as well as mind; that thought is contingent precisely on the coexistence of body and mind (*Opere* 259).[21] The ability to think is not the root cause or explanation but merely the sign of the existence of the human mind. Vico's profound Catholic faith gave substantial impetus to his search for an alternative to the sceptical *cogito* and the arid deductive logic of Descartes and the rationalists.

In *Ancient Wisdom* Vico elaborates his notion of invented truth, the *verum factum*, precisely by means of analogy to divine creation. Having established etymologically in the first paragraph that for the ancient Latins *verum* and *factum* were synonymous, Vico proposes that for the early sages the true was indeed the same as the made (*Opere* 248). Proceeding inductively, Vico bolsters this thesis by comparing human invention to divine creation, being careful first to distinguish clearly between human thinking, or *pensare*, and divine understanding, or *intendere* (*Opere* 248–9). God, furthermore, contains all the elements, both intrinsic and extrinsic, of all things within himself. He is, in effect, both inside and outside all things. The human mind, on the other hand, being external to all things save the self, can only gather the outward qualities of things. It can meditate around things but not fully take them in. To illustrate this difference, Vico suggests that God's creation, his truth, is like a three-dimensional object which is generated 'in the round' simultaneously as it is known or understood. Human truth too, is that which, in the act of being endowed with form, is known, but, in contrast to God's created truth, human truth is verisimilar; it is like a flat, two-dimensional painting rather than a sculpture (*Opere* 249).

The analogy between the creative powers of God and those of man recurs throughout *Ancient Wisdom*. It is in the human faculty of inventive wit or *ingenium* that Vico allocates this god-like talent for innovation and invention: 'just as nature generates physical things, so human wit gives birth to mechanics and, as God is nature's artificer, so man is the god of artifacts.'[22] Vico notes that in Latin, *ingenium* is synonymous with *natura*; he speculates that this is perhaps because it is the inventive faculty which distinguishes man's nature from that of the rest of creation (*Ancient Wisdom, Opere* 296; Palmer trans. 97). Ernesto Grassi has pointed out in *Renaissance Humanism* that in Virgil, Ovid, and Statius (authors whom Vico would have read), *ingenium* is linked to a 'power which determines growth, existence and passing away, ... the becoming of things' (68). Furthermore, Cicero (also required reading in Vico's epoch) clearly stipulated that *ingenium* 'unites man with the Divine'; it is the source of the *ars inveniendi*, the inventive arts, while 'ratio is the origin of the *ars judicandi*,' or the critical arts (Grassi 68). *Ingenium* is analogous to nature, therefore, in that it engenders being; it compels form out of indeterminacy. Vico also observes that in Latin *genus* refers only to the form of things; it connotes a process of categorization grounded not in the universality of abstract essences but rather in the ideality of form (*Ancient Wisdom, Opere* 261). In this brief gloss on the notion of ideal formal categories Vico takes his first cautious steps towards the theory of the fantastic or poetic universals which represents the touchstone of his new science of humanity.

In *Ancient Wisdom,* as in the oration *Study Methods,* Vico's discussion of *ingenium* is rooted in the etymology, figural attributes, and geometric associations and implications of the word *acutum,* which in English is 'acute' or 'sharp.' *Ingenium* is defined in this text as 'the faculty that connects disparate and diverse things' (*Opere* 295; Palmer trans. 96). As the remainder of this section illustrates, the underlying visual configuration here is again the acute angle with its conjoined, diverging rays. It is the most distended of obtuse angles, the ray, which is polemically juxtaposed to the acute angle and which Vico continues to exploit as the figural shorthand for his anti-Cartesian meditations.

In *Ancient Wisdom* Vico expands his speculative platform to encompass a critique of the syllogism and the sorites of classical dialectics. This was a necessary result of his burgeoning insights into the historical primacy of analogical and inductive thinking which, according to Vico, fell into disrepute only after Socrates (*Opere* 301; Palmer trans. 102). Deductive, logical methods such as the syllogism of Aristotle and the sorites or extended syllogism of Zeno only then began to make an appearance. Drawing an analogy between these later logical, deductive methods and the extension of the ray, Vico notes that rather than bringing together disparate things, the syllogism and the sorites merely draw out or extrapolate from that which is contained in the premises of the given. These methods presuppose an orderly, logical classification of reality by genus and species and these classifications remain intact and unchallenged in the process of speculation or analysis. It is a method which does not create but only elaborates and refines, rendering thought progressively more subtle and abstract in the process (*Opere* 301; Palmer trans. 102–3).

Taken to a logical extreme the syllogism and sorites emerged in Vico's time as algebra, and in the dissemination of this method, Vico discerned a serious threat to human intellectual growth. Vico feared that, as a result of the cultivation of abstract thinking, the talent for visualization would be lost and with it the ground of human inventiveness (*Opere* 303–4). In Euclidian geometry, as in inductive thinking, synthesis rather than analysis is operative; proofs are contrived by way of demonstration and combination; truth is not discovered but created (*Opere* 304; Palmer trans. 102). For Vico, the importance of Euclidian geometry lay in the fact that it did not rely on the logical ordering of abstract numbers and variables but rather on the manipulation of visible forms, and this exercise, if nothing else, 'invigorates fantasy, which is the eye of *ingenium*' (*Opere* 304; Palmer trans. 104).

Here we encounter a powerful example of the optical imagery which in *The New Science* takes on such conceptual and rhetorical importance and which is necessarily implicated in the discussion of geometric figures. The visual impact of the ray is one of outward motion and of displacement. The acute angle instead has the effect of opening up or disclosing a field or space which is both created and penetrated by the eye. A category of imagery which is clearly akin to the geometric and the optical and which is also fundamental to Vico's thought is that of light or illumination. Significantly, Vico's early description of metaphor as the most important of the 'acute sayings' and as 'a thing of remarkable splendour and a brilliant ornament in any ornate speech' links the geometric figure of the acute angle with an impression of almost blinding luminosity (*Opere* 185; Gianturco trans. 24). So, too, in the oration on *Ancient Wisdom*, Vico introduces the topos of illumination at a critical juncture in the discussion of truth and knowledge:

> knowing distinctly is a vice of the human mind, rather than a virtue, because it means knowing the limits of things. God's mind sees things in the sunlight of His truth. In other words, while it sees a thing, it knows an infinity of things along with the thing that it sees. When man's mind knows a thing distinctly, it sees it by lamplight at night. For while the mind sees it thus, the thing's circumstances are lost from its sight. (Palmer trans. 77)[23]

We may discern here the juxtaposition not only of a vivid light against a dim one, but of a single ray of light, with its limited disclosure, against the wide-angled perspective made possible by the superluminary sun. As this passage implies in its association of deductive or 'differential' knowledge with the figure of the single ray of light, the process which in humans is analogous to the engendering enlightenment of divine truth is the inductive, contextualizing, and holistic visualization of the *ingenium* represented by the acute angle.

In the oration on *Ancient Wisdom*, as in the oration on *Study Methods*, it was from the ancient art of Topics that Vico gleaned a notion of inductive thinking based on the triangular motion of dialectic. This art entails the invention of a third or middle term to act as a ligament in joining the otherwise distant and diverse (*Opere* 301; Palmer trans. 102). This third term or *argumentum* is distinct from the deductive proof or *argumentatio* of logic, for while the latter involves making manifest that which is contained in the given, the former necessitates the contriving of a new conceptual space, or common place, from which to link the otherwise removed and dissimilar. Induction rests, therefore, not on the closed circularity of logical consistency and coherence, but on the harnessing of contradiction, on the fabrication of a novel sense out of non-sense. Through the invention of a topos or commonplace, a point of reference or context is contrived from which meaning may emerge, impertinently, out of difference. This is, of course, the *modus operandi* of metaphor.[24]

Vico's anti-Cartesian and anti-rationalist polemics culminated in a work of encyclopaedic proportions and speculative range, the *Principj di scienza nuova* (in English, *The New Science*, or *NS*).[25] This text represents nothing less than an attempt to posit the true, that is, the ideal, history of human thought and human institutions, and in so doing it seeks to ferret out the very roots of distinctively human being. As Vico notes, the 'masterkey' of this new science of humanity, which cost him a lifetime of study and meditation, was the discovery that early man was 'by nature and of necessity a poet' (*NS* 34). Like the rationalists whose methods Vico had criticized, Vico had, until *The New Science*, been blinded by a scholarly conceit into assuming that the foundations of human thought lay in speculation, in the reflections of philosophers:

thus, his quest for the wisdom of the ancient Latin sages. This anachronism became manifest to Vico as a result of his cultivation of an inductive method based on observation of the particular, in this case, the particulars of human cognitive behaviour:

> It is another property of the human mind that whenever men can form no idea of distant and unknown things, they judge them by what is familiar and at hand.
>
> This axiom points to the inexhaustible source of all the errors about the principles of humanity that have been adopted by entire nations and by all the scholars. For when the former began to take notice of them and the latter to investigate them, it was on the basis of their own enlightened, cultivated, and magnificent times that they judged the origins of humanity, which must nevertheless by the nature of things have been small, crude, and quite obscure.' (NS 122–3)[26]

Having earlier traced the history of philosophy back to the inductive method of Socrates, Vico proceeds, in *The New Science*, to push his imaginative and speculative explorations back to the earliest poets and beyond, to contemplate the very first spark of human intelligence, for 'sciences must begin where their subject matters begin' (*NS* 347).

Vico describes the insights spun from this axiom in a key passage of *The New Science* which is as remarkable for the play of pivotal metaphors as for its innovative speculation:

> But in the night of thick darkness enveloping the earliest ambiguity so remote from ourselves, there shines the eternal and never failing light of a truth beyond all question: that the world of civil society has certainly been made by men, and that its principles are therefore to be found within the modifications of our own human mind. Whoever reflects on this cannot but marvel that the philosophers should have bent all their energies to the study of the world of nature, which, since God made it, He alone knows; and that they should have neglected the study of the world of nations, or civil world, which, since men have made it, men could come to know.

This aberration was a consequence of that infirmity of the human mind by which, immersed and buried in the body, it naturally inclines to take notice of bodily things, and finds the effort to attend to itself too laborious; just as the bodily eye sees all objects outside itself but needs a mirror to see itself. (*NS* 331)[27]

Next to the images of light and dark, depth and surface, interiority and exteriority, eye and focus, Vico now holds up the mirror, the glossy plane which bends the vector of vision and light back upon itself. As this philosophically charged simile underscores, it is not in nature that man may discern his reflection; nor is it nature that is being reflected in the artefacts of man. Human inventions point to nothing else but the modifications of the human mind; human institutions are the very mirror of human history (*NS* 374). From this Vico concludes that by tracing the history of human institutions with the aid of etymology and philology, one may also trace the evolution of human thought, for the 'sequence of human institutions sets the pattern for the histories of words in the various native languages' (*NS* 236).

Exploiting fully the sonority of the tradition, Vico characterizes his recapitulation of human intellectual development as a descent from the refined nature of a reflective and civilized humanity to the 'monstrous savagery' and 'unbridled bestial freedom' of a being just emerging from the feral state (*NS* 338). The topos is that of the journey from the light down into the darkness below, which is, however, the very repository and source of the light (*NS* 331). Dramatically reversing the conventional cosmologies and commonplaces, Vico also effects here a metaphysical Copernican revolution: he posits as his problematic not the question of being but rather the riddle of human becoming; his quest is for the 'masterkey' that will open the door on human historicity, on the root causes of human intellection; in short, his problem has become that of the word, not that of the thing (Grassi, *Renaissance Humanism* 115).

In keeping with mythological tradition, it is not surprising to discover that Vico employs the image of the dark and buried realm not only to refer to the remote past of human history, but also to describe the human body (*NS* 378). Once again Vico perpetrates a radical speculative reversal by turning the figural convention on its head: by positing as the original ground of human intellectual functioning the dense mass and sensory ganglia of the body, rather than the rarefied realms of the mind, Vico vindicates the body and renders its depths luminous.

Vico's inductive genius is perhaps nowhere more dazzling than in his juxtaposition of the infancy of human civilization to that of the individual human being. Although Vico amassed many precocious insights from this analogy, the most riveting and fertile was the realization that primitive man, like the infant child, is seduced into language through the senses, for 'the senses are [the] sole way of knowing things' (*NS* 374, 363). Thus, the first phase of human language, both ontogenetically and philogenetically, is mute, and consists of 'gestures and objects that have natural relations with the ideas they wish to signify (*NS* 266); in semiotic parlance, they are indexical signs of a tangible or concrete nature. The second stage on the road to abstraction and rational thought entails a transference from the tangible to the visible, from three-dimensional objects and gestures to two-dimensional graphic symbols, icons, emblems, hieroglyphs, and ideograms (*NS* 33). It is this type of visual or iconic mental activity that is still operative in man's first vocalizations, which are composed of articulated images and similitudes (*NS* 225).

Vico's basic premise is that the first utterances of *homo sapiens* were metaphorical and that metaphor, 'therefore, can be said to be a feature of the human mind that laid the foundation upon which abstract rational thought was constructed' (Danesi, *Vico* 120; 'Language' 47). This talent of early man for inventing metaphors is not founded on the recondite knowledge of sages, but is forged instead on the back of a 'robust ignorance' by means of a 'wholly corporeal imagination' (*NS* 376). Language and thought emerge from the chaotic flux of sensory experience when a first sensory experience is particularized, impressed upon consciousness and stored in the memory banks (*NS* 363). Experiential particulars become separate, distinct, and discrete, and thereby fixed in human consciousness through the contriving of an imagistic identification which becomes verbally 'embodied' in a metaphor. Reasoning by analogy from his knowledge of Western mythology and his observations of infant behaviour, Vico concludes that man first contrived distinctions among and imposed order on his sensory impressions of the world by visually construing the world as a body, that is, by forming 'the vast image of ... "Sympathetic Nature"' (NS 378). For Vico human intellection was grounded in the body both literally and metaphorically, for it was through the bodily senses that the first anthropomorphic 'ideal' and corporeal mental portraits of the world were contrived. Primarily through the operation of metaphor, early man proceeded to ascribe not just his form but also his 'sense and passion to insensate things' (NS 186), thereby creating the fables, or as Vico variously describes them, the 'imaginative universals,' 'poetic class concepts,' or 'imaginative genera,' that is, the topoi or mythopoeic mental categories which comprised the first 'mental dictionary' or 'unconscious mental grammar' of all humankind (NS 161).[28]

Vico underscores that this manner of processing reality by means of poetic class concepts or archetypes, such as Jove for the sky, Neptune for the sea, and so on, should not be misinterpreted as an intentional manipulation of symbolic levels (NS 409, 816); rather, this way of seeing represents the very condition of reality for the poetic mind. Persons or objects achieve being only insofar as they are processable through a class concept or generic character. Thus, for example, a person is not analogous to the imaginative universal; he *is* that poetic character to the extent that he shares that character's being: a warrior is not *like* Achilles – he *is* Achilles. Attributes are not abstracted and analogized; instead, 'various species of men, deeds and things' are comprised univocally under their poetic genera (NS 210).

We find in Vico's *New Science* a model of language akin to what we would describe today as a semiotic system of communication consisting not just of words, but also of gestures, objects, and hieroglyphics (Mali 172). With respect to verbal language itself, Vico isolates the four tropes as being fundamental to his 'poetic metaphysics,' namely, metaphor, metonymy, synechdoche, and, lastly, irony, which is reflective and self-conscious and thus pertains to a later, rational era.[29] But it is metaphor that Vico foregrounds as 'the most luminous and therefore the most necessary and frequent' of the figures of speech (*NS* 404).

Early humans were poets effortlessly and unconsciously, for it was out of the necessity born of ignorance and linguistic poverty that the processes implicit in metaphor, in synechdoche, and in metonymy were activated. Language was created or invented out of man's lack of understanding, for 'when man understands he extends his mind and takes in the things, but when he does not understand he makes the things out of himself and becomes them by transforming himself into them' (*NS* 405). The imagery of the ray and the acute angle surreptitiously emerge here through the verbs 'extends' and 'makes,' necessarily implicating the critique of deductive reason and the privileging of imaginative induction that have by now become coterminous, in Vico, with these figured elements of geometry.

According to Giambattista Vico the world is not discovered through language; it is called into being in language in the metaphorical identifications of the poetic genera, and gradually, through the animation and nomination of matter into a heap of 'unrelated synechdochies and metonymies' – by the invention of a 'god for each identified aspect of nature or experience' (Eco 108). Vico underscores the corporeal, sensory, and concrete ground of language and thought by noting that 'in all language the greater part of expressions relating to inanimate things are formed by metaphors from the human body and its parts and from the human senses and passions. Thus, head for top or beginning; the brow and shoulders of a hill' and so on (*NS* 405).

In postulating man's initial poetic fabulation of the world as the necessary precursor to rational and abstract thinking, Vico was the first to posit what has come to be known as the 'relativity hypothesis' of linguistics, the notion that thought and language are inextricably intertwined and evolve *pari passu*.[30] Vico proposed that thought and language are grounded in the experiences of the body, but he also argued that man's first mythopoeic thoughts and verbalizations were not the result of a merely mimetic process but rather of an inventive one. Just as childhood metaphors facilitate the transition from sensory reflection to rational thinking, so, too, humanity could not have achieved the ability to posit abstract universals and utilize prose speech without first shaping the poetic or fantastic universals in verse (*NS* 460). In effect, the personification of nature into gods and goddesses and into the heroic prototypes of bravery, cunning, and persistence represent the 'concrete' precursors of abstract concepts for, Vico says, 'in these [poetic universals], as in embryos or matrices, we have discovered the outlines of all esoteric wisdom ... in the fables the nations have in a rough way and in the language of the human senses described the beginnings of this world of sciences, which the specialized studies of scholars have since clarified for us by reasoning and generalizations' (*NS* 779).

It was essentially a process of contraction, effected in large part through generalizing metonymies and synechdochies, that caused mythopoeic constructs to be reduced and condensed into diminutive signs, and eventually into single words, much as hieroglyphs and emblems were contracted into 'a few vulgar letters' as the powers of abstraction grew and those of imagination waned (*NS* 402, 460). And, it was ignorance of the operation of these metonymic and synecdochic forces which led scholars to misconstrue the relationship between the myths and their subsequently reasoned conceptual analogues. Committing the error of anachronism, they ascribed to mythopoeic or early metaphorical thinking a veiled erudition radically antithetical to its unselfconscious and non-reflexive *modus operandi* (*NS* 402). With another of his trademark speculative sleights of hand, Vico brings home the notion that it is not reason which is veiled in poetry, myth, and metaphor, but rather that the disclosure of the real in rational or logical discourse is, insofar as it is a verbal construct, of the same ontological order as poetry; the 'real' that is disclosed is always and already a human fabrication or fabulation. 'In myth as in science that which is in itself remains inaccessible and is replaced by a mental analogue that man creates for himself whether this be an image created by fantasy or a concept established by reason' (Cantelli 289).

Vico insists that the fundamental principle of philosophy in its study of human ideas, and of philology, in its study of human words, must be the same (*NS* 429); namely, the *verum factum*, for, as Frye later puts it, 'nothing built out of words can transcend the nature and conditions of words – ratio, insofar as it is verbal, is contained in oratio' (*AC* 337). Metaphysical truth is vested in the hypothetical and ideal order of being contained in poetry, in the formal integrity of this invented world, and 'physical truth which is not in conformity with it should be considered false' (*NS* 205).

The world of objects, of phenomena, is made meaningful only to the extent that our words and thoughts make or invent a meaning or sense for it, and the mental machinery primarily responsible for this is metaphorical induction. Vico perceived in the operation of metaphor not only a way to undercut the conventional dichotomy of reason versus imagination, but also those of man versus nature, knower versus known, subject versus object. In metaphor, the distance and displacement implicit in the subject–object dichotomy of logical, denotative language is replaced by the synthesis or fusion of the creative subject with her invented worlds, worlds which in themselves constitute an ontological common-place or space and disclose an epistemological perspective. Humanity must make its truth – it is not there for the gathering. Frye, like Vico, was convinced of this, and it is this insight, together with the recognition of the central role played by metaphorical thinking in this constructive enterprise that sustains his vocation as critic and teacher. Again and again in the last phase of his writing career, from the time of *The Great Code* until his death, Frye turns to Vico and reiterates what is clearly the essence of Vico's wisdom and science: 'reality is in the world we make and not in the world we stare at' (*MM* 122).

four

Process and Freedom

In his last major publication, *The Double Vision*, Frye summarized his life's work saying,

> For the last fifty years I have been studying literature, where the organizing principles are myth, that is, story or narrative, and metaphor, that is, figured language. Here we are in a completely liberal world, the world of the free movement of the spirit. If we read a story there is no pressure to believe in it or act upon it; if we encounter metaphors in poetry, we need not worry about their factual absurdity. Literature incorporates our ideological concerns, but it devotes itself mainly to the primary ones, in both physical and spiritual forms: its fictions show human beings in the primary throes of surviving, loving, prospering, and fighting with the frustrations that block these things. It is at once a world of relaxation, where even the most terrible tragedies are still called plays, and a world of far greater intensity than ordinary life affords. In short it does everything that can be done for people except transform them. It creates a world that the spirit can live in, but it does not make us spiritual beings. (16; or, *NFR* 178)

We may detect in this passage the key markers of that second main strain in the history of critical thought that Frye described as the Longinian, creative, or psychological. As was considerably elaborated upon in *The Well-Tempered Critic* (1963), what is primarily reflected here is a concern with literature as experience, with its impact upon the reader, both individually and collectively, rather than a focus on literature 'as an object of understanding' (*WTC* 136; cf. also 113–15). In addition, there is here the suggestive Longinian echo of the word 'intensity,' the telling reference to the creation of worlds, and, finally, the inclusion of the spiritual dimension. These are aspects of Frye's construction of the poetics of process that call for close scrutiny. In this chapter I undertake this scrutiny, an undertaking which, of necessity, also calls for an exploration of Vico's contribution to Frye's notions of myth and metaphor in the context of the poetics of process.

It is not to be wondered at that another set of terms enlisted by Frye to trace the contrastive zone in the history of critical theory is that of 'Romantic' versus 'Classical' (*WTC* 114). Frye associates the Romantic with an emphasis on psychology and traces the tradition back to Plato, although he insists that the chief ancient spokesman for this meta-school of criticism is Longinus (*WTC* 115). The next step in this juxtaposing of the Aristotelian and Longinian traditions in Frye's critical thought gives a strong indication of the manner in which Vico is embroiled in the unfolding of the Longinian or Romantic strain and deserves to be quoted:

This emphasis [in the Longinian tradition] is psychological rather than esthetic, and is based on participation rather than on detachment. It thinks of a poem as an 'expression,' to use Croce's term, rather than as Aristotle's *techne* or artifact, and its fundamental conception, corresponding to 'imitation' [in the Aristotelian tradition], is 'creation,' a metaphor which relates the poet to his context in nature. (*WTC* 115)

The shadow of Vico is cast here not just because of the reference to Croce, himself a great student of Vico and an important disseminator of his thought during the first half of the twentieth century, but also because of the emphasis on creation rather than imitation.[1] As I set out in the preceding chapter, Vico's understanding of the mythopoeic mind-set constitutes the foundation or ground for the *verum factum* principle, a principle that Frye had also encountered in Blake.[2] It was not until Frye turned his attention specifically to the Bible, in writing *The Great Code,* that he explicitly tackled Vico's 'ideal eternal history,' the science of becoming human. This is not to deny that, as my preceding occasional comments have suggested, there is a strong Vichian strain in *Anatomy.* We may note, particularly in the First Essay entitled 'Historical Criticism: Theory of Modes,' and in the Third Essay, 'Archetypal Criticism: Theory of Myth,' a parallelism of emphasis and argument to the 'ideal eternal history' traced by Vico in *The New Science.* And, although there is no explicit acknowledgment of Vico in this text, there are key points of contact which call for attention.[3]

In his First Essay, 'Historical Criticism: Theory of Modes,' Frye observes that European fiction has, during the past fifteen centuries, moved progressively through five modes, and that the same general pattern can be traced in classical literature in a greatly foreshortened form (*AC* 35). The first literary mode, both historically and thematically, is the mythic one, wherein the hero is projected as a god having powers superior in kind and degree both to man and the natural environment. Here the protagonist is a kind of divine being with unqualified freedom. The second phase, the romantic, is typified by a protagonist who has powers superior only in degree to other men and to nature; to this mode belong the marvellous tales of heroic exploits. The third mode, which Frye labels the 'high mimetic,' is characterized by a protagonist who is a leader, that is, superior to the ordinary man, but not to the environment, and who is, therefore, subject to both criticism and defeat. The hero here is not above the order and law of nature. The low mimetic mode posits the experiences of the protagonist as those of the ordinary mortal and is frequently present in comedy and realistic fiction. Last to evolve is the ironic mode, wherein the protagonist is portrayed and perceived as in some sense inferior in power and intelligence to the ordinary reader, as somehow captive in a frustrating or absurd cosmos which allows very little freedom of choice and action (*AC* 33). The general progression that emerges in moving through this sequence of modes is from greatest to least freedom and from a lack of realism to verisimilitude until the sequence turns back to myth through irony. Frye himself notes that this 'modal' and historical approach to criticism essentially reflects a quasi-organic rhythm of cultural aging, where the production of culture (as distinct from its consumption) may be, like ritual, 'a half-involuntary imitation of organic rhythms or processes,' as artists imitate their predecessors but in progressively more sophisticated ways, producing a tradition of cultural aging 'which goes on until some large change interrupts the process and starts it over again' (AC 343). Here, as in the Third Essay, the emphasis is on the displacements or transitions that may be detected in the various modes and periods of literary production, from the most idealized and imaginary or mythical to more realistic, mimetic or verisimilar literary works.[4]

The parallels between this section of *Anatomy*, which Frye calls 'historical criticism,' and Vico's 'ideal eternal history' are noteworthy. Frye's modes of literature are, in effect, reflections of the intellectual situations or mental attitudes prevailing in generally identifiable historical periods. Vico's three recurring ages are also theoretical categorizations of trends or patterns in human intellectual and social development over time, marked by a revolving progression from the primitive, god-centred society ruled by oracle, on through to the imaginative age of heroes wherein a superior aristocracy is dominant, to the age of men, an age 'in which all men recognized themselves as equal in human nature' (*NS* 31). There is in both paradigms a pattern of increasing self-consciousness or reflexivity in human thought, a pattern which Vico emphasizes in his theories on the evolution of language.

Vico associates with his mythic phase or age of gods a 'mute language of signs and physical objects,' namely, the hieroglyphic; to the heroic phase he assigns a language spoken by means of 'heroic emblems or similitudes, comparisons, images, metaphors and natural descriptions,' namely, the symbolic; and to the age of men he assigns 'a language whereby people may fix the meaning of the laws' and which 'served the common uses of life,' namely, the vulgar (*NS* 32). Vico's schema is a morphological one similar to Frye's organic model, for nations and their civil institutions, including their languages, arise, develop, mature, decline, and fall (*NS* 349). According to Vico, early humans, like children, were incapable of thinking in an abstract, or rational manner; instead they utilized 'imaginative class concepts' or 'poetic characters' or 'imaginative universals' to which all particulars which resembled them were reduced (*NS* 209). From this infantile state of visual thinking, of categorical thinking by means of corporeal images, a thinking based on the senses rather than on the reflective or analytical faculties, humans gradually evolved through the second or adolescent phase of 'perceiving with a troubled and agitated spirit' and finally entered the mature last stage when they 're-flected with a clear mind' (*NS* 33).

Frye and Vico have both projected a primitive humanity cower-ing before the forces of nature (see, for example, *NS* 339, *EI* 22). This uneasy rapport between humanity and the non-human mate-rial order is the underlying factor that shapes all cultural pro-duction. Hans Blumenberg, in commenting on Vico and his understanding of the function of myth, underscores the human transformation or sublimation of fear into poetry, of the 'shiver' into 'song,' and suggests that through Vico, and in the 'middle of the century of the Enlightenment,' the romantic thesis that 'gen-ius (*ingenium*) creates the possibility of human life, by introducing institutions and ordinances, figures and boundaries, into reality' is already established (379). Hayden White, too, identifies Vico's great insight to be the perception that 'the problem ... was to uncover the implicit rationality in even the most irrational of human imaginings, insofar as such imaginings had actually served as the basis for the construction of social and cultural institutions by which men had been able to live their lives both *with* and *against* nature itself' (52).

Frye, as we have seen, opposes the romantic (Longinian) theory of criticism to the classical (Aristotelian) theory and insists that at the base of this distinction is a fundamental divergence in the attitude to nature. The Aristotelian approach, based on imitation, views nature as the context of the poem or work; it turns nature into an object, into what Coleridge called *natura naturata*, an objectified nature which the artistic product seeks to emulate or reproduce or mirror (*WTC* 115–16). The creative or Longinian tradition views cultural production not as a spectator sport but as a process of world-making which engages not only the artist, but also the cosmos and the reader. Nature, now not *naturata* but *naturans*, is considered as a 'total creative process of which the poet's creation forms a part' (*WTC* 116), and the focus is thus not on the commodity or product that is manufactured in culture, but on the *interpenetrating processes* that culture, and life itself, entail. Nature, in this paradigm, is not the object of observation but a multi-faceted interactive force, organic and changing, alive and responsive – in short, not an 'it' but a 'Thou,' to co-opt Martin Buber's terminology.[5] Already in an early paper first published in 1958, entitled 'Nature and Homer,' Frye saw the crucial element in the Longinian critical paradigm to be its view or perspective on nature:

> Of course nature is the environment as well as the content of art, and in that respect will always be external to it. That is why the figure of the mirror has been so frequently employed to illustrate the relationship. But the indispensable axiom that, as long as we are talking about art, nature is inside art as its content, not outside it as its model, was written once for all into the critic's handbook by Longinus when he identified the 'sublime,' not with size, but with the mental capacity that appreciates the vastness of nature and, in the stock but expressive phrase, 'takes it in.' (*FI* 42)

In effect, we may detect a crucial distinction between the Aristotelian and Longinian traditions in criticism to be coterminal with the conceptual or modal distance that separates the mythopoeic mind-set from that of the last stage in both Vico's ideal eternal history and Frye's sequence of historical modes. The vector along which this sequence of changes unfolds is, as Frye elaborates in *The Great Code*, one that traces the changes that human history generally follows in its unfolding rapport with nature and in its corresponding notions of truth. What is also incorporated in the notion of displacement that is implicit in Vico and explicitly elaborated by Frye is the principle that the move towards rationalism, analytical thinking, and 'objective' truth is essentially incompatible with the passionate, intense experience of the sublime which is firmly entrenched in the first phase of language.

The course which humanity is seen to run involves a gradual transition from an outward-looking sensory orientation towards nature's being to a more introverted mind-centred perspective, one perhaps best summarized by Descartes's *cogito*. This process both reflects and defines the modulations in the dominant literary modes and styles, for just as human thinking moves from the metaphorical and the concrete to the analytical and the abstract, so, too, literature proceeds from the mythic and from verse to the realistic and demotic and to prose. Vico is very explicit about this process, saying, 'by a necessity of human nature, poetic style arose before prose style; just as, by the same necessity, the fables, or imaginative universals, arose before the rational or philosophical universals which were formed through the medium of prose speech' (*NS* 460).

The general progression that emerges in moving through Frye's sequence of modes is from greatest to least freedom and from a lack of realism to verisimilitude, until the sequence bottoms out again with the ironic mode. Here, there is a turning away from a concern with accurate representation of the everyday but in the opposite direction from myth; that is, instead of positing a realm of ideality and complete freedom the ironic mode, as delineated by Frye, posits an absence of freedom and extreme scepticism regarding the very feasibility of the ideal. It is after this turn to irony that the mode of myth makes its reappearance as the cycle starts again.

Irony or the ironic phase takes on a critical role here and represents the transitional mode associated with the turn or, rather, return or *ricorso* back to the free imaginative play of myth and metaphor. In Vico as in Frye, irony denotes a type of decadence, a decline which precedes a rebirth. Vico denigrates irony as 'falsehood by dint of a reflection which wears the mask of truth' and opposes it to the 'true narrations' of the first gentiles (*NS* 408). In the conclusion to *The New Science*, he emphatically associates the 'false eloquence' of irony with 'corruption' and describes the transition from *corso* to *ricorso* as a sequence of two barbarisms:

the 'barbarism of reflection,' marked by 'subtleties of malicious wits' and 'base savagery, under soft words,' and the 'barbarism of sense,' which is a 'generous savagery' marked by 'primitive simplicity' and people who are 'again religious, truthful, and faithful' (*NS* 1102, 1106).

Frye, too, considers the predominance of irony to mark the dying gasp of realism or the mimetic as culture returns to the seminal orbit of myth (*AC* 42). Indeed, Frye's theory of displacement posits irony as the signal that myth in its pure or ascendant form is about to recur: 'Reading forward in history, therefore, we may think of our romantic, high mimetic and low mimetic modes as a series of *displaced* myths, *mythoi* or plot formulas progressively moving over towards the opposite pole of verisimilitude, and then, with irony, beginning to move back' (*AC* 52). In *The Educated Imagination* Frye posits an explanation for this proximity between myth and irony, suggesting that both are cultural modalities which lead the reader to a holistic or universalistic perception of the world. Irony involves a detachment of the imagination from the world the characters live in, resulting in a world view which is clear and 'in the round,' while myth projects, through the imagination, a portrait not of an individual hero, 'but a great smouldering force of human desire and frustration and discontent, something we all have in us too, part of mankind as a whole' (*EI* 25). What I would add as well is that paradox is at the heart of both irony and metaphor, and thus may serve as the modal bridge between the demonic or nihilistic version of paradox entailed in irony which rests on an imbalance and division, or as Wayne Booth describes it, 'the vertiginous but finally delightful discovery of depth below depth' (*Rhetoric of Irony* 177), and the paradox of metaphor which is not 'subtractive' but is instead a way of synthesizing difference, of forging a nexus out of a negation through the 'is and is not' of metaphor's copula.

Peter Hughes has noted that irony is central to *The New Science*, where 'the rhetoric of enlightenment increasingly clashes with the enormities, absurdities, and extremes that it relates' ('Creativity and History' 166). This represents the recognition of the presence in Vico of that intentional intellectual posturing which he,

Vico, condemns so roundly as 'la boria dei dotti,' the conceit of scholars (*NS* 517, 518). What Hughes does *not* observe is the additional presence in *The New Science* of the re-emerging mythic perspective which Frye describes as being typical of the ironic mode: 'The return of irony to myth that we noted in fiction is paralleled by some tendencies of the ironic craftsman to return to the oracular. This tendency is often accompanied by cyclical theories of history which help to rationalize the idea of a return, the appearance of such theories being a typical phenomenon of the ironic mode' (*AC* 62). In Vico's *New Science* the return is not only that of the ironic craftsman re-entering the oracular orbit; there is also a re-emergence of the mythical in a literary or poetic sense, as we see in the myth of the 'ideal eternal history.' Frye insisted that art deals not with the real but with the conceivable. If the 'eternal history' is true, it is so in the sense in which the first poetic Jove myths which Vico describes were true, that is, in the Platonic sense of being 'ideal' or in Frye's sense of being conceivable. Vico considers the poetic truth contained in myths to be metaphysical truth: 'These fables are ideal truths suited to the merit of those of whom the vulgar tell them; and such falseness to fact as they contain consists simply in failure to give their subjects their due. So that, if we consider the matter well, poetic truth is metaphysical truth, and physical truth which is not in conformity with it should be considered false' (*NS* 205).[6]

Vico insisted that human knowledge of nature is limited to the 'certain' in that it consists only of outward knowledge or sensorially acquired data and is not the true knowledge from origins that can only accompany an act of making. Since humanity has created culture, but not nature, knowledge *per causas*, knowledge of the true, is limited to the realm of human production, to the artistic constructs, scientific paradigms, and other facets of humanity's culture or world-building processes. For Frye as for Vico, all literature, indeed all culture, descends from myth, and the process that explains the various phases or versions of cultural production is one that Frye, borrowing the lexicon of Freud, calls 'displacement.' What Frye understands by this term is the gradual tendency observable in literature over time to move away from the pole of fiction and make-believe towards that of plausibility and 'realism.' The changes entailed in this movement involve the transition from the realm of fulfilled desire, of imaginative freedom to conjure the most ideal and visionary projections, to one where anxieties and concerns with time, contingency, nature, and fact are so pressing as to contrive a veritable imaginative prison or hell. The tendency, once followed to its full expression, becomes so extreme, so exaggerated, that the plausible has been again left behind and the demonic side of the imagination makes its radical appearance through the nihilism of the most ironic and bleak satires and tragedies.

In the Second Essay of *Anatomy*, 'Ethical Criticism: Theory of Symbols,' Frye undertakes a consideration of the manner in which language may generate various levels of meaning. Taking the medieval theories of polysemy as recorded and developed by Dante as his point of departure, Frye sets forth a comprehensive review of how words mean, how they lead to interpretations. As was the case in the First Essay on modes, the order or sequence of the arrangement is important. Briefly, the first level is the literal one. Here the word functions primarily as motif and the main concern is not with external reference but with the internal integrity of the verbal pattern created within an individual text. It corresponds to the ironic phase. The second level is the descriptive one wherein the word operates as sign in a mirroring or referential type of relationship. The reality principle is strong here and language is used instrumentally, striving for accuracy and precision of re-presentation. The third level, the formal one, utilizes the word primarily as image in the context of allegorical meaning.

But it is the fourth and fifth levels that we are primarily concerned with. The mythical level utilizes the word as archetype, which Frye describes as 'a universally communicable symbol,' one that exists in a social context, which forms part of established conventions emerging out of common human desires. Literature that is most deeply engaged in the archetypal phase of symbolism impresses a reader as primitive and popular precisely because it is motivated by the fundamental and universal human desires – the primary needs for food, shelter, freedom, and companionship. The last phase, the anagogic, is typified by the word as monad, a radical metaphorical use of language which incorporates an ecstatic experience, a state of rupture and rapture in which the mind experiences itself as both containing, and contained by, the world; there is here the experience of a kind of epiphany in which the world is not objectified as other but experienced as interpenetrative complement and completion.

What is of particular interest in this essay is the emergence again of a tendency to proceed from constraint to freedom. The lower-level and presumably less 'ethical' uses of language, namely, the literal, the descriptive, and the formal, seem to impose limits, are somehow confined and accountable to something other and elsewhere, and are thus limited in their potential impact upon the reader. In the archetypal realm we enter the literary universe proper, where works of literature look only to each other, while in the last level, the barriers not only of form and culture have been erased, but also those of time, space, and consciousness itself. What must be stressed here is that again, as in the First Essay, Frye sees the pre-eminent vector defining cultural change to be related to freedom, and the realm of greatest freedom is associated, once again, with myth and metaphor.

It is not surprising, in view of this observation, to find that the Third Essay, 'Archetypal Criticism: Theory of Myths,' is really an elaboration of the last two types of literary activity in the theory of symbols, for 'the structural principles of literature ... are to be derived from archetypal and anagogic criticism, the only kinds that assume a larger context of literature as a whole' (*AC* 134). The primary sources for the archetypal symbols of Western literature are, for Frye, the Bible and classical mythology. Thus it is from here that Frye culls his grammar of literary archetypes. In this Third Essay, then, a schematic account is given of the structure of archetypal imagery considered from the perspectives of meaning and of narrative shape or pattern. The structures and identifying traits of the basic narrative patterns or *mythoi* cannot here be analysed in depth. It is sufficient to note that there are four such basic narrative patterns: romance, comedy, tragedy, and irony. Again, freedom emerges as the important distinguishing quality, for romance and comedy are associated with the attainment of liberty, with a move away from the fetters of circumstance, of time and place, and from the inhibitions of law, both natural and otherwise. At the opposite pole, tragedy and irony are seen to be linked to a downward spiral, to the world of jaded expectations, a fall into the grip of fate, fact, and finality.

The Fourth Essay, 'Rhetorical Criticism: Theory of Genres,' is an effort to define the main genres of literature, which Frye lists as drama, epos, fiction, and lyric. These are discussed on the basis of their forms and their rhythms. The essay then addresses the specific variations within each of these genres, and it is the last section of the essay that may properly be described as a 'rhetoric,' for it deals with the interconnections between the world of words and the world of social action or *praxis* on the one hand, and the world of individual thought on the other (*AC* 326). In this section it is again apparent that the subject matter of criticism is not just the literary universe but the sphere of human culture as a whole. It is also again made clear that any attempt to approach the work of criticism as being only the disinterested dissection of an aesthetic object must necessarily fall short of the mark.

Frye concludes his Fourth Essay, and indeed *Anatomy* as a whole, with a meditation on rhetoric which is radically Viconian in that it suggests that the conventional privileging of discursive reason, of dialectic, in Western culture has been grossly misconceived: 'nothing built out of words can transcend the nature and conditions of words, and ... the nature and conditions of *ratio*, so far as *ratio* is verbal, are contained by *oratio*' (*AC* 337). This emphasis on the rhetorical aspect of language will become, as we shall see, of key importance in Frye's subsequent elaboration of the poetics of process.

Vico described his work as *scientia*, that is, as an ordered, ideational structure of general propositions. This is the same concept of science that underlies Frye's appeals for a disciplined literary criticism, one that is causal rather casual, systematic rather than random (*AC* 7–8). Vico also describes his history of human cultural phases as 'ideal,' that is, as a mental construct or system. Frye

describes his own metacritical review of literary criticism as an
'anatomy,' that is, by his own definition, a 'creative treatment of
exhaustive erudition' (*AC* 311), 'a vision of the world in terms of a
single intellectual pattern' (*AC* 310). In other words, he considers
it to be, like Vico's ideal eternal history, a unified mental construct or system.

What is to be underscored here is that there are no claims being
made for any objective truth or precise correspondence between
the paradigmatic treatments of culture or criticism that are presented by our authors and an accessible existential reality. Science, no less than myth is, as Frye says in the 1975 essay 'Expanding
Eyes,' a verbal construct, and the disclosure of the real in logical
or analogical discourse is, in so far as it is a verbal construct, of the
same order as poetry. The real that is disclosed in words is always
and already a human fabrication. Regardless of the formal domain of human conceptual activity, all such operations are con-
ducted through mental analogues that we generate for ourselves.
In critical discourse, as in art, it is inevitably a formal, hypothetical
statement that is made.

In the Tentative Conclusion to *Anatomy* Frye is very clear about
delineating the limitations of the aesthetic or formalist approach
to criticism. Having arrived at the proposition that no verbal
structure is free of rhetorical elements, Frye goes on to state that
'our literary universe has expanded into a verbal universe, and no
aesthetic principle of self-containment will work' (*AC* 350). Instead, taking a perspective that is, like Vico's, radically Longinian
and humanistic, Frye makes the link between the constructed
universe of words and the ethical realm of *praxis*: 'No discussion
of beauty can confine itself to the formal relations of the isolated
work of art; it must consider, too, the participation of the work of
art in the vision of the goal of social effort, the idea of complete
and classless civilization' (*AC* 348). Frye is explicit that in order
for art and criticism to attain this vision, both must move beyond
the 'aesthetic or contemplative aspect of art,' and it is archetypal
criticism, which Frye deems the most useful in this regard, for it
treats art as 'an ethical instrument, participating in the work of
civilization' (*AC* 349). A.C. Hamilton has pointed out, quite rightly,

that *Anatomy* concludes with an insistence on the radically hypothetical nature of literary works (252n13). This is precisely where Frye picks up the main lines of his critical discourse in *The Great Code*, where he attempts to fully explore the implications of the statement that 'It is the function of literature ... not to run away from the actual, but to see the dimension of the possible in the actual' (*GC* 49). In turning now to *The Great Code* and to Frye's most exhaustive treatment of myth and metaphor, I embark as well on an examination of his fullest exploration of the implications of what is essentially Vico's *verum factum* principle.[7]

five

Process, Concern, and
Interpenetration

As we saw in our brief survey of *Anatomy*, Frye's claims for the function of myth are substantial: poetic mythology is nothing less than the 'concrete, sensational, figurative, anthropomorphic basis out of which the informing concepts of discursive thought come' (*FI* 58; cf. *AC* 352). In staking out this pre-eminent role for myth in the shaping of human cultural production, Frye has, some curious inconsistencies notwithstanding, acknowledged his indebtedness to Giambattista Vico, 'one of the few thinkers to understand anything of the historical role of the poetic impulse in civilization as a whole' (*CP* 34). With reference to these inconsistencies, we have seen that in *The Great Code* of 1982, Frye states that although Vico's theory of linguistic modes was his point of departure, there was very little left of Vico in what finally emerged (65). He then proceeds to note that the influence was more pronounced in the *Anatomy of Criticism* of 1957, a text which makes no reference to Vico in its index and only alludes in passing to Joyce's 'Viconian theory of history' (62). This is even more curious in view of the numerous entries, noted above, in Frye's private papers confirming the pre-eminence of Vico as guide for the 'third book.' Particularly noteworthy is the following entry: 'I imagine the third book will be heavily indebted to Vico, as heavily as an author can be who, like necessity, knows no law. I know of no other thinker who is as close to thinking of the entire structure of concern as a poetic myth' (NB 19, par. 343). Finally, in the introductory chapter of *Words with Power* (*WP*) of 1990, Frye states without hesitation that '*The Great Code* owed a good deal to Vico' (xii).

Vico's influence is more openly and more generously acknowledged by Frye in the last productive phase of his writing life. We note, for example, that in *Words with Power* he describes Vico as 'the discoverer of the principle that all verbal structures descend from mythological origins.' Further, Frye goes on to observe that Vico's axiom was '*verum factum*: what is true for us is what we have made' (82). Frye unequivocally proceeds to call this principle the 'essential axiom of criticism' (135). Some years earlier, in an important essay that focuses primarily on Vico and that is tellingly entitled 'The Responsibilities of the Critic' (1976), Frye describes Vico as having entertained 'a great vision of the development of social institutions out of what he called "poetic wisdom," or an original mythology' (*MM* 129). But, contrast this statement to the following observations in *Words with Power*:

> *The Great Code* owed a good deal to Vico, the first modern thinker to understand that all major verbal structures have descended historically from poetic and mythological ones. But even Vico had a limited interest in the continuous social function of literature, and he paid little attention to the principle that makes it insistent. (xii–xiii)

My contention here is that, on the contrary, Vico was quite concerned with the social function of literature, and that the *verum factum* principle, which is the philosophical ground for the poetics of process in Vico, as in Frye, is precisely the principle that 'makes it insistent.'

What is undeniable, however, is the importance of the Viconian strain in Frye's attempts to negotiate his way along the critical path of process that he had proposed in concluding *Anatomy* – in his attempts, in other words, to 'reforge the broken links between creation and knowledge, art and science, myth and concept' (*AC* 354). This critical path must be seen to engage myth and myth's key tropological vehicle, metaphor, in a central way, and, as we may conclude from the emphasis on the social context, it is a criticism increasingly engaged with literature as a constructive process rather than as an aesthetic product.

Frye has examined many facets of the word 'myth' and its variations, and we may note in *The Great Code*, as in the earlier *Anatomy*, a concerted attempt to draw neat distinctions among the various possible usages of the word 'myth,' particularly in its literary and critical context. We may begin by considering Frye's definition of myth in the glossary of *Anatomy*, where he provides the following explanation:

> Myth: A narrative in which some characters are superhuman beings who do things that 'happen only in stories'; hence, a conventionalized or stylized narrative not fully adapted to plausibility or 'realism.'

We also find a more technical list of definitions for the term *mythos*, related to the various critical modalities explored in *Anatomy* and already surveyed above. In *The Great Code*, which represents an extended meditation on myth and metaphor, particularly as applied to the context and cultural impact of the Bible, the emphasis noted earlier in Frye's exploration of myth and its association with freedom is sustained and substantially enlarged upon. Indeed, *The Great Code* may well be seen to represent an elaborate and sustained reflection on the literary, social, ethical, and religious importance of the Exodus myth, the myth of freedom.

In the first chapter of *The Great Code*, wherein Vico is explicitly invoked, language is broken down into three primary uses or phases that closely parallel the distinctions of Vico's ideal eternal history. Frye uses this *theoria* and overview of language's modulations as a point of departure for his study of the linguistic diversity and range found in the Bible. Frye insists, first of all, that although not identical to literature, the Bible is close to literature in that its language is dominated by metaphor and its structure shaped by myth. The three Vichian phases as described here by Frye are the familiar mythopoeic or metaphorical one, the allegorical or metonymic, and the final descriptive or ironic. Frye replaces Vico's terminology for these phases (the poetic, heroic, and vulgar) with the terms hieroglyphic, hieratic, and demotic (*GC* 5), but in essence they are the same.

The crucial contribution that Frye does make to this paradigm is the addition of the category of *kerygma* as the psycho-linguistic modality particularly represented in the Bible. This category of language is the place in Frye's critical universe where faith and vision converge, and it will be given more detailed consideration presently. What is important at this juncture is to emphasize that it is based on mythical structures and metaphorical language; that it constitutes the extreme or radical functioning of such poetic processes and thus represents a major critical elaboration of Frye's early intuition that '... religion and art are the two most important phenomena in the world; or rather the most important phenomenon, for they are basically the same thing. They constitute, in fact, the only reality of existence ...' (letter to Helen Kemp, 23 April 1935, *NFHK* 1:425–6).[1]

The reality that subtends existence and that Frye associates with art and religion is that of recreative energy, the energy that is employed in turning human existence from passive reception and observation into lively relational engagement and co-creation. In surveying the modulations of language in chapter 1 of *The Great Code*, Frye sought to demonstrate that God is dead only because entombed in a dead language, in a fossilized, objectified, immobilized representational projection:

> we might come closer to what is meant in the Bible by the word 'God' if we understood it as a verb, and not a verb of simple asserted existence but a verb implying a process accomplishing itself. This would involve trying to think our way back to a conception of language in which words were words of power, conveying primarily the sense of forces and energies rather than analogues of physical bodies. (17)

David Cook, exploring Frye's thought in the context of the Canadian liberal imagination, notes that the energy Frye associates with this resurrected conception of God is the relational power harnessed by mythopoeic language through the recreative and regenerative force of metaphorical thinking (41).

This leads us to the crucial distinction Frye makes between mythology and ideology, a distinction not always recognized by other theorists of culture and literary critics. This distinction is one implicit in Vico's privileging of the poetic word, in his insistence on the primacy of the mythopoeic mind-set. Like Vico, Frye has consistently maintained that 'Man lives not directly or nakedly in nature like the animals, but within a mythological universe, a body of assumptions and beliefs developed from his existential concerns' (*GC* xviii). Mythology, unlike ideology, is based on those concerns, or to use a Freudian term, anxieties, that are primary, that unite all humanity. These primary concerns are perennially listed by Frye as the basic desires for life, freedom, love, and happiness. Here, then, is where Frye derives his second and important definition of the word 'myth' in *The Great Code*. The first usage was the conventional Aristotelian one of myth as '*mythos*, plot, narrative, or in general the sequential ordering of words (*GC* 31). More to the point, for Frye certain such narratives take on a special status; they serve a special social function in that 'they are the stories that tell a society what is important for it to know' (*GC* 32–3). Mythologies, which derive from primitive societies, but which continue to operate behind or beyond our present ideologies, are expressions of primary concerns for food, shelter, survival, love, and freedom. For Frye, ideology is the distortion of myth, for while both are expressions of social concern, the former is primarily a 'rationalization of authority' and is thus militant and aggressive, and, by extension, divisive rather than unifying: 'Every ideology, because it is or includes ... the rationalizing of a claim to social authority, tries to get itself established as the right or "orthodox" one' (*MM* 103).[2] As I have argued elsewhere, there is a major difference between Frye and many left-leaning critics of culture (such as Roland Barthes) that arises out of Frye's refusal to conflate mythology and ideology.[3] Frye persisted in this distinction throughout his career and argued vehemently against any such process as the 'demythologization' propounded by particular poststructuralist and postmodernist critics: 'I see it as the essential task of the literary critic to distinguish ideology from myth, to help reconstitute a myth as a language, and to put literature in its proper cultural place as the central link of communication between society and the vision of its primary concerns' (*MM* 103).

Literature is directly engaged with mythological structures, with the generation and regeneration of a primary link between the mind and the world. Ideology entails a second layer of concerns and preoccupations which are superimposed on this foundation (*MM* 91). The language of myth is the language of identity reflecting 'an intimacy with the environment which emerges in the metaphorical structures of poetry,' and it inheres in an ideal, 'unfallen' or non-alienated state of consciousness. In the case of ideology, however, language is essentially used metonymically, to urge that a 'particular structure of authority is the closest we can get to the ideal one, ... [it] is being "put for" the ideal' (*MM* 90). Presumably, this progression may be extended to the realm of irony, where even the possibility of projecting the ideal through language is instead replaced by the sense of 'a fatal asymmetry between the processes of reality and *any* verbal characterization of those processes' (White, *Metahistory* 232). The ironic mode and mentality is one often accompanied by a sense of futility and sterility, by the 'utter failure of nerve' that starts off the *ricorso*. What the *ricorso* describes, then, is that twist in the road of human spiritual becoming where the ideology of a demonic aesthetic, with its excessive and cynical exercise of power and profound moral bankruptcy, is left behind as humanity progresses through the jaded futility and loss of the ironic mode to again emerge in the realm of myth, the world peopled by gods (*MM* 134).

For Vico, poetry, the turn to myth and metaphor, represents the first category of human responses to the world; it is the first of a series of approaches that humanity takes in its attempt to confer meaning on reality, and of necessity this involves a subjective act of mental creation for, '[b]ecause of the indefinite nature of the human mind, whenever it is lost in ignorance man makes himself the measure of all things' (*NS* 120). The act of imagining through myths is thus the first psycho-linguistic process by means of which humanity constructs its reality, and what Vico centres this process on, in direct parallel to Frye's association of myth with primary concerns, is the *sensus communis*, the essential and universal common sense that binds communities.

Sensus communis, writes Vico, is 'judgment without reflection, shared by an entire class, an entire people, an entire nation, or the entire human race' (*NS* 142). Vico elaborates on the universality of the *sensus communis*, saying:

> Uniform ideas originating among entire peoples unknown to each other must have a common ground of truth. This axiom is a great principle which establishes the common sense of the human race as the criterion taught to the nations by divine providence to define what is certain in the natural law of the gentes. And the nations reach this certainty by recognizing the underlying agreements which, despite variations in detail, obtain among them in respect to this law. (*NS* 144–5)

John D. Schaeffer in his extensive study of the concept of *sensus communis* in Vico emphasizes that this type of judgment is not reflective or individual, but rather represents the 'common ground of truth,' and that this is communal or social in nature and is constituted by the 'underlying agreements' that bind human communities (*Sensus Communis* 84). Vico links this community-based consensus to mythopoeic language in a very direct way: 'There must in the nature of human institutions be a mental language common to all nations, which uniformly grasps the substance of things feasible in human social life and expresses it with as many diverse modifications as these same things may have diverse aspects' (*NS* 161).

The mental dictionary that Vico refers to here is comprised of poetic characters or 'fantastic universals,' the poetic genera or commonplaces that the mythopoeic mind contrives in giving human sense to the material world (*NS* 402, 404). Frye posits a similar body of archetypes or universal metaphors, usually taking the form of a god related to some particular aspect of nature, and representing the basic building blocks or fundamental recurring imaginative structures in the human imagination (*GC* 48; *AC* 118). For Vico as for Frye, these basic metaphors or mythopoeic units arise from, and are an expression of, the most fundamental and universal of human concerns and aspirations (*NS* 145, MM 101–3).

For Vico, myths are *vera narratio*, or true narrations, in that they give expression to fundamental principles of social life; they express an ideal or general truth about the human condition and are not specific, historical accounts of past events disguised or allegorized under a veil of poetry as certain scholars had wrongly surmised. The mythopoeic mind-set utilizes imaginative universals or poetic characters as a means of perceiving and giving human meaning to external reality; these represent the first stage by which the mind orders the chaotic flux of sensory stimuli through a categorizing and generalizing process based on a primal perception of identity. Metaphor is the means by which identity is originally achieved in perception: 'It is the form perception most immediately takes. Metaphor is the first of the tropes and the first of the operations of mind in the act of knowing' (Donald Phillip Verene, qtd. in Mali 180).

Both Vico and Frye base their privileging of the mythopoeic mode on the radical metaphoricity of the psycho-linguistic processes that are implicated in this mental stance. This results in large part because the phase of mythopoiesis is also the most radically free in its possibilities for autopoiesis; it is the mental mode or phase least constrained by a notion of truth based on imitation or reference to a normative, external objectivized order and the most exuberant in its expression of subjective desire, of internal states and structures that are essential to and define what it is to be human. For Vico as for Frye the task of mythmakers is precisely to project in their poetic characters the basic ideals of humanity in the face of a potentially mundane and compromised day-to-day reality. In effect, the task is to ensure that the original shock of being made self-aware that Vico captured in the primal scene and in the description of the mythopoeic projection of the thundering sky-father is recreated, relived. This primal metaphor, this imaginative universal which represents humanity's entry into culture, 'fuses the origin of language, religion, and community in a metaphor that organizes and interprets sense data ... [it]

creates human self-consciousness by suspending the flux of sensation, fixing sensation in time and projecting it into external reality' (Schaeffer 90). As the inclusion of thunder, lightning, the
deity, and the emotional intensity of sexuality in this primal scene
suggest, the experience that accompanies the invention of religion, law, and language is, in effect, the experience of the sublime, an experience rooted in the paradox of self distinct from,
yet connected to, the larger whole – part of and yet apart from the
cosmos.

Frye was very preoccupied in the last phase of his career, the
phase that I claim he dedicated primarily (though not exclusively)
to delineating in a detailed way the critical theory of process, with
the Vichian theory of psycho-linguistic modes and their relation
to truth. When we follow Frye in his re-elaboration of Vico's
phases of language, we see that the main focus is to emphasize the
variability, not only in linguistic usage, but also in the very model
of 'truth' that accompanies the various phases and variations of
what the French semioticians call *langage* or a metalinguistic semiotic system. In introducing chapter 1 of *The Great Code*, Frye asks
himself whether it is possible to trace a history of *langage*, 'a
sequence of modes of more or less translatable structures in
words, cutting across the variety of *langues* employed, affected and
conditioned but not wholly determined by them' (5).

This is, of course, precisely what Vico had sought to accomplish
in his ideal eternal history, which Frye uses as his point of departure in tracing his own ideal history of language modes. As was the
case in *Anatomy*, there is here a movement from the mythopoeic
mind-set to the mimetic, from the predominance of metaphorical
identity to allegorical metonymies and on to the descriptive and
ironic modes of thinking and speaking.

The early poetic or hieroglyphic phase is one in which language
evinces no clear mental separation between the subject and the
world; rather, there is a 'feeling that subject and object are linked
by a common power or energy' (*GC* 6). There is a fundamental
sense of unity between humanity and nature, as is suggested by the
predominance of mythical or poetic characters or 'gods' which
embody the unity of human personality and some aspect of the

natural world. The mental operations engaged here are not abstractive or analytical but 'concrete' and very much grounded in the senses and, as Vico well understood, in the operation of memory.[4]

The second or hieratic phase involves an epistemological move towards the separation of subject and object as the 'intellectual operations of the mind become distinguishable from the emotional operations and abstraction and logic emerge' (*GC* 7). David Cook summarizes the fundamental differences entailed in this modality as follows:

> it is the beginning of continuous prose as opposed to the discontinuous aphorisms that characterize the pre-Socratics ... this prose can be conceived of on a dialectical basis in its attempt to form a transcendent world as opposed to sensual world that predominates in metaphorical language ... the development of hieratic continuous prose allows for the development of monotheism in the place of the polytheistic world of nature. (38)

This dialectical, syllogistic, and metonymic type of thinking, which Frye sees as culminating in thinkers such as Kant who focus on a phenomenal world rather than the world of 'things in themselves' (*GC* 12) is eventually replaced by the third phase, Vico's 'vulgar' or, as Frye renames it, demotic phase. Here there is a clear separation of subject and object as the objective order of the world, assembled by the mind in an inductive reflective or mirroring fashion, replaces the deductive mode of accessing 'the true.'

As Frye summarizes in a dizzying fashion, such a notion of referential, descriptive, mimetic truth of correspondence has today itself been substantially undermined. The insights of Copernicus, Darwin, and Einstein, among others, have exposed the extent to which the so-called objective observations of science were projections of a particular mental perspective or mode of thinking and not a one-to-one mapping of the 'real' onto the conceptual. Frye makes an important reference to Whitehead at this point in his discussion, and it is here that the philosophical, or rather, theological, substratum of his use of the word 'process'

makes its appearance and deserves careful attention and lengthy
reiteration:

> What I am concerned with at present is not the question whether
> God is dead or obsolete, but with the question of what resources of
> language may be dead or obsolete. The metaphorical and metonymic
> phases of language have been in large measure outgrown because
> of the obvious limitations that they imposed on the human mind.
> But it seems clear that the descriptive phase also has limitations, in
> a world where its distinction of subject and object so often does not
> work ... For third-phase writing, founded as it is on a sense-appre-
> hended distinction between objects that are there and objects that
> are not, 'God' can only go into the illusory class. But perhaps this
> kind of noun-thinking is, at least here, a fallacy of the type that
> Whitehead calls a fallacy of misplaced concreteness. (*GC* 17)

Frye's allusion to Whitehead's 'fallacy of misplaced concreteness'
(*Science and the Modern World* 51, 58) is, of course, a reference to
the notion, so central to the poetics of process, that language in its
kerygmatic function has much more to do with processes and
energies than with things or products, just as in Whitehead's
science of process, the post-Einsteinian universe has more to do
with energies and relations than with fixities of matter.

Frye turns next to a particular passage of the Bible which is of
interest not only because of its theological importance but because of its curious linguistic turn:

> In Exodus 3:14, though God also gives himself a name, he defines
> himself (according to the AV) as 'I am that I am,' which scholars say
> is more accurately rendered 'I will be what I will be.' That is, we
> might come closer to what is meant in the Bible by the word 'God' if
> we understand it as a verb, and not a verb of simple asserted
> existence but a verb implying a process accomplishing itself. This
> would involve trying to think our way back to a conception of
> language in which words were words of power, conveying primarily
> the sense of forces and energies rather than analogues of physical
> bodies. To some extent this would be a reversion to the metaphori-

cal language of primitive communities ... But it would also be oddly contemporary with post-Einsteinian physics, where atoms and electrons are no longer thought of as things but rather as traces of processes. (*GC* 17–8)[5]

In his private writings, Frye acknowledged that he saw his own contributions to criticism as parallel to the accomplishments of Einstein in the physical sciences: 'criticism of the humanities is bankrupt, as Newtonian physics was in 1900, and ... Frye represents the beginning of a nuclear period in criticism' (NB 7, par. 100). This 'nuclear' period in criticism found early and profound inspiration in the ideas of Whitehead, as Robert D. Denham has traced in his careful review of the notion of interpenetration in Frye's private and published writings.[6]

Alfred North Whitehead was profoundly aware of the implications of the revolutionary insights of Einstein and Darwin, and Whitehead's published meditations on the philosophical and theological aspects of these implications formed the basis of an important anti-materialist movement in Christian theology which came to be known as 'process theology.' Process theology rests on a privileging of organicism; underpinning this organicism is the notion of interpenetration, the awareness of the inevitable interrelatedness of all things in the universe and the conviction that the independent existence of entities is impossible. 'Process' in this sense taps into established philosophical traditions which include Buddhism and the ideas of Heraclitus among its more ancient manifestations, and Bergson, Peirce, and especially Whitehead and Teilhard de Chardin more recently (Lowe 4).[7] As Frye acknowledged in his private writings, Plotinus is another of the pivotal classical process thinkers.[8] In metaphorical terms which converge with currently circulating images of Gaia, and which harken back to Blake's cosmological poetic constructs, the universe is likened to a quickened organic multiplicity which, in its unity, constitutes the body of God – a unity, furthermore, which is mirrored in the individual and particular, the chain of being implicit and contained in each of its elements – 'a universe in a grain of sand.' Blake himself may clearly be given a place in the chronicles of the history of this theological/philosophical vein in Western thought, and Frye's extensive work on Blake early in his scholarly career created a fertile ground for the ideas of both Whitehead and Giambattista Vico, another pivotal 'process' thinker. As was noted, Buddhism represents an important and very ancient manifestation of process philosophy and its touchstone principle of interpenetration. Although a full and detailed exploration of the influence of Buddhism and Eastern thinking on Frye is yet to be undertaken, preliminary studies confirm the early and unquestionable exposure of Frye to Eastern philosphical traditions.[9]

Frye makes frequent use of this notion of 'interpenetration' in contexts which often evoke the thought of both Martin Buber and Alfred North Whitehead. We see this in *The Great Code*, for example, when, in the course of discussing radical or anagogic metaphor, he describes the 'infinite mutual fusion or penetration of all things, each with its individuality yet with something universal in it,' involving as it does the sense of 'annihilating ... space and time as we know them' (168). Later, in *The Double Vision* (1991), Frye elaborates on this point and is even more explicit with respect to the influence of Whitehead: 'The first book of philosophy that I read purely on my own and purely for pleasure was Whitehead's *Science and the Modern World*, and I can still remember the exhilaration I felt when I came to the passage: "In a certain sense, everything is everywhere at all times. For every location involves an aspect of itself in every other location. Thus every spatio-temporal standpoint mirrors the world." This was my initiation into what Christianity means by spiritual vision' (40–1; or, *NFR* 198). Frye's privileging of the mythopoeic mind-set may be understood in this context, for it is this mental stance which most closely approximates, at the subjective level of individual human experience, the cosmic interpenetration that is the basic principle underlying both Frye's criticism of process and Whitehead's process theology.

It is the facility that mythopoeic language has to harness and sustain relational processes that represents the basis for Frye's theological and ethical commitment to the poetic word. For Frye, the *logos*, the Word, is connected to the rhetorical power of language, its ability to project us into the living paradoxical experience of singularity within a unity of variety and multiplicity. The kerygmatic power of the poetic word also rests on the capacity it has to project ideal, or at least better worlds, and to generate sufficient enthusiasm about these possible worlds that creative processes are set in motion. As Longinus well knew, this power reaches its most intense pitch through the metaphorical constructs of mythopoeic language, and thus it is not surprising to find that, for Frye, it is the 'primary function of literature, more particularly of poetry, to keep re-creating the first or metaphorical phase of language during the domination of the later phases, to keep presenting it to us as a model of language that we must never be allowed to underestimate, much less lose sight of' (GC 23).

The radically relational metaphors of poetry, those that tend to emphasize while at the same time bridging the existential distance or abyss between the self and the world, constitute a key aspect of this mode of linguistic functioning (WP 85).[10] Frye concludes his exploration of language's modal possibilities with the suggestion that the language of the Bible is really an extreme version of the mythopoeic mode in that it combines the intense intersubjectivity of the first poetic psycho-linguistic stage with a radically rhetorical, that is, oratorical or proclamatory dimension. For Frye, in contrast to Bultmann, kerygma cannot be disassociated from myth, for kerygma, like myth, entails a persistent recreation or projection of essential concern, in Vico's words, of the sensus communis, and the positing of a potential program of action for the satisfaction of those concerns.[11] What the mythopoeic foundation of kerygma represents is the liberation of humanity from the chains of inevitability, with the insistent reminder that truth is made, not observed. It persistently calls to us and calls us to create again that more ideal home which all those universally discoverable myths about paradise tell us we must try to contrive since we have conceived them. The creative processes of poetic language are a reminder that human limits are defined, not by the actual, but by the conceivable, and that anything we have the power to conceive we have the hope of bringing to actuality. For Frye this is the ethical axiom of the criticism of process but it is also, of course, the essence of his religious faith which he, like the author of the epistle to the Hebrews, defines as the '*hypostasis* [substance] of things hoped for and the *elenchos* [evidence] of things not seen' (*MM* 99; or *NFR* 349).

Clearly, the ideal of freedom plays a crucial role in this formulation of a process-based poetic theology, for, in electing to make those choices which contribute to the stratum of the universe which is human history and culture (Frye's 'envelope of culture' or what another process thinker, Teilhard de Chardin, called the 'noosphere'), all other aspects of the cosmos must, perforce, be affected. The key lessons of both process poetics and process theology, with their touchstone principle of interpenetration, underscore the cosmic seriousness of humanity's engagement with the god-like freedom to create.

Conclusion:

The Ethics and *Praxis* of Process

I have been attempting to clarify the distinction to be made in Northrop Frye's critical writings between the criticism of process and the criticism of product. The criticism of process, my main focus of interest, is that critical approach which engages literature as experience rather than literature as an object to be anatomized and analysed. Within this 'process' sphere of critical activity, Frye included that centrifugal and interpenetrative orientation of thought which moves between the total world of possibility that is literature and that world which may, in one sense, be seen to enclose this realm, and yet also be enclosed by it – the realm of the actual (*GC* 49). In the previous chapter, I suggested that the rhetorical power of *kerygma* represents a crucial linking function that language may acquire in facilitating the interplay of energies between these spheres. In concluding my examination of Frye's criticism of process, I want to look briefly at the ethical and pragmatic dimensions implicit in this critical perspective.

In a *New York Review of Books* article on *Words with Power, The Double Vision, Reading the World,* and *Myth and Metaphor,* Denis Donoghue writes that if we do indeed live in an age when '"the destiny of man presents its meanings in political terms," then there is no hope for Frye's books' (9 April 1992). He goes on to say with respect to these books that, 'If we took them seriously we would have to change our lives' (28). What I want to stress in closing is precisely this point – that Frye was very much concerned with the here and now, that he was all too aware of the historical baggage with which the present moment is invested, and, like Vico, engaged in a defence of the critical enterprise precisely because he sought to insist on the fact that change is real, as is choice. For both thinkers, the literary enterprise, and more particularly, that special experience of literature which, since Longinus, we have associated with the word 'sublime,' is crucially linked to the project of constructing possibilities for an improved, more just and humane world, a vision clearly rooted in the humanistic tradition.

Frye and Vico were both educators, and not isolated writers working in seclusion from the world of *praxis*; indeed, they were rather all too aware of their role in shaping the next crop of society builders. That 'evangelical fervour' which, according to A.C. Hamilton, sets Frye off from most critics (ix), may also be detected in Vico's inaugural orations, in his *Autobiography*, and especially in *The New Science* itself.[1] As Donald Phillip Verene discusses at length in the introduction to the volume *On Humanistic Education* (1993),[2] Vico's main pedagogical claim, one deeply rooted in the *querelles* of the ancients and the moderns, was that invention, not syllogistic clarity, should be the first priority in the education of youth. In Frye's writings on education, and particularly in *The Educated Imagination* of 1963, we encounter parallel arguments in that it is, ultimately, the *social* utility of the literary arts that is underscored.

For Vico, as for Frye, the importance of the experience of sublimity in the cultivation of the student's mind and character was indubitable. In the essay on Dante which has come to be known as 'La discoverta del vero Dante' ('The Discovery of the True Dante'),[3] Vico discusses Longinus's main sources of sublimity as being, first, nobility of soul, and secondly, a mind informed by public virtues (*Opere* 952). In the oration of 1732 entitled *De Mente Heroica* or *On the Heroic Mind* Vico makes a direct link between the 'heroic' life and the sublime, and connects both to that quality of the human mind which is linked to the divine. He writes, 'The human mind which, because of its similar nature, derives much satisfaction from contemplating the divine, the infinite and eternal, cannot but meditate on the sublime, cannot but attempt the great, cannot but achieve distinction' (*Opere* 912; my translation). Donald Phillip Verene has emphasized that, in defending a mode of education which cultivates imagination and memory, Vico was prompted by the belief in the constructive possibilities of an education that did not sacrifice the paradox and mystery of the whole of human experience to the false security of the logical method:

> The search for truth has classically always placed the human in relation to something beyond the reach of any method or form of self-contained, step-by-step thinking and analyzing. The self's search for truth has commonly prized *ingenium* (the perception of connections among what otherwise seem separate) over method; imagination (as the power to form true images) over abstraction and classification; and reason (as the metaphysical attempt to know fully) over ratiocination (as process of intellectual ordering of specific content). (*On Humanistic Education* 2)

The focus on the 'total education of humanity' that Vico's work represents, particularly in *The New Science*, is closely linked, Verene tells us, to the Greek ideal of *paideia*, a conception of education that stresses the complete development of the human spirit to a point where it may participate fully in the human world of culture and civil affairs (14).

Domenico Pietropaolo, in discussing Frye, has linked this notion of *paideia* to freedom and to Matthew Arnold's conception of 'culture' ('Northrop Frye e la paideia della libertà' 1992). If we turn to the essay entitled 'The Critical Discipline' we find that Frye explains Arnold's conception of culture as 'the higher society of art and science which shows us what humanity *can* do' (*OE* 32; my emphasis). This conception is one that premises the projection of possibility, through culture, as the precondition for human progress towards a world more truly human and humane; it is a profoundly humanistic conception of the socially progressive function of culture, one that Vico most assuredly shared. As Pietropaolo notes, Frye was consistent in his loyalty to this Arnoldian tenet (403–4). In chapter 3 of *Fearful Symmetry*, entitled

'Beyond Good and Evil,' Frye was already exploring the workings of the imagination as a prerequisite for action (55), while in *Anatomy* he explicitly stated that 'the ethical purpose of a liberal education is to liberate, which can only mean to make one capable of conceiving society as free, classless, and urbane' (347). *Anatomy* may be seen, furthermore, to have an underlying organizational and thematic thread which is profoundly linked to this preoccupation with liberation. As I suggested earlier, the principal vector along which all categories in all four essays of *Anatomy* may be distinguished is the vector of freedom.

It was well past the days of *Anatomy*, and only on closer acquaintance with Vico's thought, that Frye was able to articulate a philosophically grounded defence of this conviction on the basis of the *verum factum* principle. And it was in developing this Vichian strain in his thinking that Frye was able to substantially, if implicitly, address the critiques of those who associate him with an anti-utilitarian, impractical, and utopian/romantic (in the worst possible sense) stance. I have in mind here, for example, the critique of Barbara Herrnstein Smith in *Contingencies of Value* (1988). For Herrnstein Smith, Frye is an anti-utilitarian humanist/redemptionist who conforms to the highs and lows of traditional cultural distinctions while engaging in the 'double discourse of value,' that is, in the forked-tongued denial that evaluation has a place in criticism.[4] In her critique, Herrnstein Smith does not recognize the crucial influence of Vico on Frye. The result is that the proximity between Herrnstein Smith's own utilitarian relativism and Frye's Vichian constructivism goes unnoticed and unaccounted for, and Frye is essentially stereotyped as a somewhat out-dated and out-of-touch 'high-brow' romantic.[5]

John Fekete is another critic who, arguing instead from a materialistic perspective, nevertheless fails to explore the significant implications of the Vichian strain in Frye's critical orientation.[6] In his critique of Frye, we encounter the usual and unflattering use of words such as 'idealist,' 'transcendent,' and 'high priest' to summarize Frye's alleged place in the critical field (*Critical Twilight* 111, 126). He raises the objection that Frye does not confront 'real history' (whatever that might be) and that he leaves the material world 'unchanged' (118).[7] How such an attack can be levelled against someone with Frye's publication record and world-wide influence is mystifying, to say the least;[8] however, the short-sightedness of Fekete's critique goes beyond such ideologically motivated claims. In reading *Anatomy*, Fekete summarizes Frye's crucial distinctions between catharsis and 'ecstasis' by saying that in Frye there is 'the abolition of *catharsis*, the shock of subjectivity in the confrontation of aesthetic immediacy with everyday imme-diacy, in favour of *ecstasis*, the vision of innocence accessible sym-bolically ... this symbolic ecstasy is substituted for the transformation of material reality, in such a way as to obscure the real historical possibility of realizing this ecstasy in the everyday life of real human beings' (121). That Fekete is positing the reification of some aesthetic experiences (see his idiosyncratic description of *catharsis*) and not others seems to be the logical conclusion to be drawn from this passage. That there is no possible link between the experience of the symbolic and the experience of the 'every-day of real human beings' emerges as another, quite astounding, implicit conclusion that may be drawn.

Perhaps Herrnstein Smith best summarizes the underlying prob-lematic here, namely, that Fekete forgets that he, like Frye, is, despite his repeated appeals to 'empirical' and 'objective' reality, *constructing* an account or an argument, a critical perspective, and, as Herrnstein Smith and Frye *both* acknowledge, 'There is no account ... that *as such*, will eradicate or transcend other people's significantly *different* identities/economies/perspectives and will make them, autonomous subjects that they *also* are, willing to forego their own interests, desires, and advantages' (Herrnstein Smith, *Contingencies of Value* 177). Northrop Frye, his preference for the figural paradigms of biblical typology rather than Herrnstein Smith's marketplace metaphorics notwithstanding, also made es-sentially the same point, namely, that to be aware of our condi-tioned state is not to say that this can be purged (*AC* 19). As Herrnstein Smith says, if a critical theory 'is understood as [an] analysis that strives and claims to expose ideology or false con-sciousness and thereby to reveal the true, underlying, *actual* work-ings of the present state of affairs or system,' then such a notion of critical theory suffers from 'epistemological asymmetry' and should be abandoned (*Contingencies of Value* 173). Fekete's argument would appear to fall into this very category of critical thinking.

Frye's own Aristotelian taxonomies and interpretive models make no claim to any status but that of metacriticism, and as Frye in good Vichian manner accepts, criticism, at whatever level, is poetic in nature, and is itself prone to take on the same, conditioned narrative outlines as myth and fable (*AC* 12, 29). As the nature of *Anatomy of Criticism* (a metacritical taxonomy of critical approaches to literature) itself implicitly suggests, Frye, like Herrnstein Smith, rejects the 'epistemological asymmetry' of critical theories that claim, not the status of opinion, but that of truth.[9] The pluralistic tolerance that subtends the critical thinking of both Frye and Herrnstein Smith may, in Frye's own terms, be seen as the very hallmark of 'ethical criticism'; namely, as that 'transvaluational ability to look at contemporary social values with the detachment of one who is able to compare them *in some degree* with the infinite vision of possibilities presented by culture' (*AC* 348; my emphasis). Indeed, 'culture' is itself defined by Frye as the 'totality of vision of possibilities,' and as the 'body of imaginative hypotheses in a society,' hypotheses that extend beyond the 'naturally possible and morally acceptable' (*AC* 127). While Frye and Herrnstein Smith agree with Bourdieu that cultural goods arise as a result of the exercise of evaluative authority by particular members of a community, and not as the result of any intrinsic quality that such goods may possess (see, for example, *AC* 345; *Contingencies of Value* 32), both also accept the operation of individual and class interests in this very process of evaluation (*AC* 346–7). Herrnstein Smith relies primarily on the model of the economic system to describe the operations or interactions that are entailed in the 'negotiation, transformation and redistribution of value,' while Frye couches his analysis in the political vocabulary historically associated with concepts of economic free play, namely, liberalism and its commitment to individual emancipation (*AC* 347–8).

Herrnstein Smith, like the rhetorical neo-humanists and like the poststructuralists, follows a well-beaten path away from metaphysics with its taint of objective truth, turning instead towards language as the meandering common place for infinite revisionings of truth. But, unlike many contemporary theorists, and in accord with both Vico and Frye, Herrnstein Smith is not cast by the telegraphic model of communication into despair over a failed vision of linguistic unity – into a notion of language such as Frederic Jameson's prison house, for example, relentlessly blocking exchange between the self and the world. Instead, she adopts a pragmatic or rhetorical 'instrumental' model in which language is comprised of verbal acts that serve to mobilize the subject by connecting her, however provisionally and temporarily, to specific other active and reactive sectors of the world. Instead of the hermetic seal of language, we have language as a contrived and contriving common market where reciprocity between any given individual and the world with its multiplicity of other individuals is rendered possible and attainable, if admittedly not perfectible.

Wayne Booth has noted the link between pluralism and the rhetorical or instrumental model of language, while also stressing the social dynamics implicit in such a non-objectivist configuration: 'For the traditional cognitive ends, they [most contemporary pluralists] substitute practical or rhetorical effects on readers and societies, on 'pedagogical communities' (*Critical Understanding* 215). In such models of language negotiation and adaptability are central, for as Herrnstein Smith has remarked, there is always a tug-of-war in language between epistemic or hermeneutic stasis and change (*Contingencies of Value* 123). As the Fourth Essay in *Anatomy*, entitled, fittingly enough, 'Rhetorical Criticism,' explicitly sets out, Frye must be seen to belong within this group of non-objectivists: 'nothing built out of words can transcend the nature and conditions of words, and ... the nature and conditions of *ratio*, so far as *ratio* is verbal, are contained by *oratio*' (337). Vico insisted that his work was one of *scientia*, that is, an ordered, ideational structure of general propositions. This is the same concept of 'science' that underlies Frye's insistence on the creativity of critical thought. Vico describes his history of human cultural phases as 'ideal,' that is, as a mental construct or model. Frye describes his own metacritical review of literary criticism as an 'anatomy,' that is, a 'creative treatment of exhaustive erudition' (311), a 'vision of the world in terms of a single intellectual pattern' (310). In other words, he, too, considers it to be a unified mental construct or model.

In the work of Vico and Frye, as in the writings of Barbara Herrnstein Smith, there are no claims being made for any objective truth or precise correspondence between the paradigmatic treatments of culture or criticism that are presented and a stable, fixed, and accessible objective reality. Further, Frye, like Whitehead, sees science as dealing not with static reified objects, but with subjective events, experiences, or occasions. Indeed, for all of these thinkers, the notion of 'realism' must be seen, in Herrnstein Smith's words, as a 'little masterpiece of question begging': Whose reality? When and under what circumstances? We do not and cannot live in direct, unmediated contact with the world around us – what we can do, and according to all of these concerned thinkers, what we should do, is experience radically the mediating creativity of the mind. This is brought about through the intensification of the experience of being that great criticism, like great art, is able to facilitate.

Jonathan Hart concluded, in a review of Frye's last few books published in 1992, that 'A vision of freedom seems to be the end that Frye asks of literature and criticism' ('Frye's Anatomizing' 128). I would modify this observation by adding that, for Frye, freedom is the beginning of criticism as well as its end. Frye writes in *The Great Code* that

> man is a child of the word as well as a child of nature, and just as he is conditioned by nature, and finds his conception of necessity in it, so the first thing he finds in the community of the word is the charter of his freedom. (22)

Since the beginning of humanity's poetic adventure there have been ways of using words that intensify our experience of being, our consciousness, and as Longinus, Vico, and Frye have underscored, language achieves its most intense pitch through the paradoxes of metaphor. The most extreme mode of such language is what Frye calls 'kerygmatic,' and what this encompasses is the Longinian notion of ecstasy, of subjective experiences and processes that take one out of oneself and are associated, because of their great intensity and urgency, with prophetic or oracular experiences (*WP* 100–15). Vico provided Frye with the crucial link between the Longinian notion of sublimity and the concept of recreation through the *verum factum* principle. Frye's exploration of kerygmatic linguistic process incorporated the intense emotional and intellectual engagement of the sublime, an experience that is, as Frye says, 'exhilarating rather than humiliating' (*DV* 35; or *NFR* 194), with an ethical imperative to act (*WP* 115–16). Incorporating the principle from Shelley's *Defence of Poetry* that all creative endeavour is part of a total effort or project that continually reconfigures the goals of human work, Frye insists that cultural production is an ethical act, one that serves to shape the range, and the reach, of human possibility.

That this view and the critical perspective that subtends it is at the core of the poetics of process is made emphatic at the end of *Anatomy* where Frye refers to the Second Essay on 'Ethical Criticism,' saying:

> We tried to show in the second essay that the moment we go from the individual work of art to the sense of a total form of the art, the art becomes no longer an object of aesthetic contemplation but an ethical instrument, participating in the work of civilization. (349)

It has been easy for some to misconstrue Frye's references to 'the total form of art' or the 'total body of human culture' as representing a closed, monolithic entity or unity.[10] Such a view would be quite antithetical to Frye's process approach to poetics and to its philosophical footing, the *verum factum* principle. This view emphasizes nothing if not the infinite scope or creative potential of human imagination to conjure and contrive. In a sense, this brings Frye close to Mikhail Bakhtin, who, in his preoccupation with the relationship between the mind and the world, opted much more for 'the Kantian heterogeneity of ends' rather than the 'Neo-Kantian lust for unity' (Michael Holquist, *Art and Answer-*

ability xv). In Bakhtin, where the emphasis is on 'perception as an act of authoring' (xv), one distinctly senses the kind of Vichian reverberations that are explicitly evoked in such comments of Frye's as 'reality is in the world we make and not in the world we stare at' (*MM* 122) and 'what is true we have made true' (*WP* 135).

That the reader or listener is the focus of process poetics must be stressed, for any view of art that is concerned with *praxis* and possibility must have at its heart a preoccupation with the role of the recipient in realizing the potential that the reading process may unleash from the text. In *The Great Code*, where Frye undertook a first exposition of *kerygma*, the relationship is described using the metaphor cluster of the bride and groom:

> Wherever we have love we have the possibility of sexual symbolism. The *kerygma*, or proclaiming rhetoric, of the Bible is a welcoming and approaching rhetoric, addressed by a symbolically male God to a symbolically female body of readers. Coming the other way is the body of human imaginative response, as we have it in literature and the arts, where the language is purely imaginative and hence hypothetical. (231)

Kerygmatic writing, the writing that attempts to go beyond 'the limitations of literature into a different kind of identity with readers' (*WP* 116) – writings like those of Dostoevsky, Kierkegaard, Nietzsche, Kafka, and Sartre (and I would add to Frye's list other examples such as Emily Dickinson, Emily Brontë, and Flannery O'Connor) – all have a profoundly challenging and intense form of address that makes them part of a secular scripture. Engagement in such reading processes propels readers beyond the 'ideological,' as Frye defines this term, in its connection to secondary concerns (those that have to do with the institutionalization and the self-promotion of power structures) and back to preoccupations that are primary – issues related to fundamental freedoms and rights which flow from a belief in the sanctity and dignity of life.

Frye explicitly links such kerygmatic writing to Longinus and the sublime when he writes that in order to understand the processes that are operative in this mode of address we need 'the guidance of a critic who understands what we have called the ecstatic state of response, and the difference between the ideological rhetoric that persuades and the proclamation that takes us out of ourselves' (*WP* 111). The best of these critics, says Frye, is Longinus, and the most intense kerygmatic state of consciousness is what Frye calls 'spiritual' (128). What this modality entails is an experience of reality that may be achieved through mythopoeic writing. The view of reality that is constructed through such usages of language is 'neither objective nor subjective, but essentially both at once, and would of course leave the old opposition of idealism and materialism a long way behind' (*WP* 128).

Frye unequivocally concluded that the one essential axiom of criticism is Vico's *verum factum* (*WP* 135). Implicit in the *verum factum* principle, and in Frye's Longinian notion of *kerygma*, is the realization that the sublime response is triggered *not* by the denial of the chains that bind us, but by our capacity to take in, and yet project ourselves beyond, the fundamentally constrained, contingent nature of our being. It is the determination to create in the face of this 'givenness,' to persistently engage in the business of *making* meaning that emerges as the ethical imperative and heroic dimension of Frye's notion of process. It is in this determination that we may see the critical interface between Barbara Herrnstein Smith's romantic relativism and the Longinian constructivism of Vico and of Frye. The criticism of process is, then, that very wide, extremely heterogeneous branch of the critical enterprise which goes beyond the mechanics of the construction of verbal artefacts to consider the way in which the power of words has been, is, and may yet be played out in the making of our worlds.

Notes

Introduction: Beyond the Great Divide

1 For some critical variations on this theme see John Fekete, 'Northrop Frye: A Critical Theory of Capitulation,' *The Critical Twilight: Explorations in Ideology of Anglo-American Literary Theory from Eliot to McLuhan* (London: Routledge and Kegan Paul, 1977) 107–31; W.K. Wimsatt, 'Criticism as Myth,' *Northrop Frye in Modern Criticism*, ed. Murray Krieger (New York: Columbia UP, 1966) 75–107; and E.D. Hirsch, 'Literary Evaluation as Knowledge,' *Contemporary Literature* 9 (Summer 1968): 319–31.

2 Robert D. Denham, 'Auguries of Influence,' *Visionary Poetics: Essays on Northrop Frye's Criticism*, ed. Robert D. Denham and Thomas Willard (New York: Peter Lang, 1991) 77–99.

3 For a current assessment of Frye's influence see Robert D. Denham, 'Auguries,' and the proceedings of an international conference held at Victoria University in the University of Toronto, 29–31 October 1992, published as *The Legacy of Northrop Frye*, ed. Alvin A. Lee and Robert D. Denham (Toronto: U of Toronto P, 1994). See also *Rereading Frye: The Published and Unpublished Works*, ed. David Boyd and Imre Salusinszky (Toronto: U of Toronto P, 1999).

4 See, for example, Theodor W. Adorno, *Aesthetic Theory* (London: Routledge and Kegan Paul, 1984); Pierre Bourdieu, *La Distinction: Critique social du jugement* (Paris: Les Éditions de Minuit, 1979); Jacques Derrida, *The Truth in Painting*, trans. Geoff Bennington and Ian McLeod (Chicago: U of Chicago P, 1987); Thomas Weiskel, *The Romantic Sublime: Studies in the Structure and Psychology of Transcendence* (Baltimore: Johns Hopkins UP, 1975); Neil Hertz, *The End of the Line: Essays in the Psychoanalysis of the Sublime* (New York: Columbia UP, 1985); Jean-François Lyotard, *L'Inhumain: Causeries sur le*

temps (Paris: Éditions Galilee, 1988); Terry Eagleton, *The Ideology of the Aesthetic* (Cambridge, MA: Basil Blackwell, 1990); Frances Ferguson, *Solitude and the Sublime: Romanticism and the Aesthetics of Individuation* (New York: Routledge, 1992); *The Sublime: A Reader in British Eighteenth-Century Aesthetic Theory,* ed. Andrew Ashfield and Peter de Bolla (New York: Cambridge UP, 1996).

5 See, for example, Paul de Man, *Blindness and Insight: Essays in the Rhetoric of Contemporary Criticism* (New York: Oxford UP, 1971); Gianni Vattimo, *La fine della modernità* (Milano: Garzanti, 1985); Jurgen Habermas, *The Philosophical Discourse of Modernity: Twelve Lectures,* trans. Frederick Lawrence (Cambridge, MA: MIT P, 1992); and Jean-François Lyotard, *The Postmodern Condition: A Report on Knowledge,* trans. Geoff Bennington and Brian Massumi (Minneapolis: U of Minnesota P, 1984).

6 For a concise discussion of the place of the sublime in the contemporary discourses of modernity and postmodernity see Jean-François Lyotard, *The Postmodern Condition: A Report on Knowledge*; and 'Answering the Question: What is Postmodernism?' trans. Regis Durand, vol. 10 in the series 'Theory and History of Literature,' ed. Wlad Godzich and Jochen Schulte-Sasse (Minneapolis: U of Minnesota P, 1984).

7 All translations from the Italian are my own unless otherwise indicated.

8 The most comprehensive and current bibliography is that of Robert D. Denham, *Northrop Frye: An Annotated Bibliography of Primary and Secondary Sources* (Toronto: U of Toronto P, 1990). See also Denham's periodic updates in the *Northrop Frye Newsletter,* edited and published by Denham. For an overview of Frye criticism, see A.C. Hamilton, *Northrop Frye: Anatomy of his Criticism* (Toronto: U of Toronto P, 1990), esp. ch 1, and *The Legacy of Northrop Frye.*

9 For a brief discussion of Frye and Derrida on the question of the 'centre,' see A.C. Hamilton, *Northrop Frye: Anatomy of his Criticism* 278n43; and Ian Balfour, 'Can the Centre Hold? Northrop Frye and the Spirit of the World,' *Essays in Canadian Writing* 7/8 (Fall 1977): 214–21. See also Donald R. Riccomini, 'Northrop Frye and Structuralism: Identity and Difference,' *University of Toronto Quarterly* 49 (Fall 1979): 33–47; Paul Ricoeur, '*Anatomy of Criticism* or the Order of Paradigms,' *Centre and Labyrinth: Essays in Honour of Northrop Frye,* ed. Eleanor Cook et al. (Toronto: U of Toronto P in association with Victoria Univ., 1983) 1–13; Michael Dolzani, 'The Infernal Method: Northrop Frye and Contemporary Criticism,' *Centre and Labyrinth* 59–68; and Robert D. Denham, 'An Anatomy of Frye's Influence,' *American Review of Canadian Studies* 14 (Spring 1984) 1–19, esp. 3–6.

10 'Towards Defining an Age of Sensibility,' *ELH, A Journal of English Literary*

History 23.2 (June 1956): 144–52; rpt. in *Fables of Identity: Studies in Poetic Mythology* (New York: Harcourt, Brace and World, 1963) 130–7. *Anatomy of Criticism: Four Essays* (Princeton, NJ: Princeton UP, 1957) 65–7.

11 See, for example, A.C. Hamilton, *Northrop Frye: Anatomy of his Criticism* 184; Frank Lentricchia, *After the New Criticism* (Chicago: U of Chicago P, 1980) 15; Robert D. Denham, *Northrop Frye and Critical Method* (University Park: Pennsylvania State UP, 1978) ix; and Geoffrey Hartman, 'Ghostlier Demarcations,' *Northrop Frye in Modern Criticism* 121.

12 See also Domenico Pietropaolo, 'Frye, Blake, e la boria dei dotti,' *Allegoria: per uno studio materialistico della letteratura* 1.3 (1989): 134–8 for a discussion of Frye's distinction between critical discourse and literature.

13 See, for example, Frank Kermode, 'Northrop Frye,' *Puzzles and Epiphanies: Essays and Reviews, 1958–1961* (London: Routledge and Kegan Paul, 1962) 73; and René Wellek, 'The Poet as Critic, the Critic as Poet, the Poet-Critic,' *Discriminations: Further Concepts of Criticism* (New Haven: Yale UP, 1970) 257–8.

14 I owe the choice of this apt expression, if not its application, to Eric Rothstein, 'Anatomy and Bionomics of Criticism: Eighteenth-Century Cases,' *Eighteenth-Century Studies* 24.2 (Winter 1990–1): 197, special issue on 'Northrop Frye and Eighteenth-Century Studies,' ed. Howard D. Weinbrot.

15 All references to Northrop Frye's unpublished papers and notebooks are based on information kindly provided by Robert D. Denham and Michael Dolzani, who are currently editing Frye's papers in preparation for publication as part of the Collected Edition of the Works of Northrop Frye, forthcoming from the University of Toronto Press. These documents form part of the 'Northrop Frye Papers' collection at Victoria University in the University of Toronto. Passages cited from Notebook 19 will be published in *The 'Third Book' Notebooks of Northrop Frye, 1964–1972: The Critical Comedy*, ed. Michael Dolzani (Toronto: U of Toronto P, forthcoming).

16 Although research on Vico and Frye will be more thoroughly canvassed below, among the attempts to address this topic have been the following: Ian Balfour, *Northrop Frye* (Boston: Twayne, 1988) 90–2; Domenico Pietropaolo, 'Frye, Vico, and the Grounding of Literature and Criticism,' *Ritratto di Northrop Frye*, ed. Agostino Lombardo (Rome: Bulzoni, 1990) 87–101; and Nella Cotrupi, 'Verum Factum: Viconian Markers along Frye's Path,' *The Legacy of Northrop Frye* 286–95. See also the important early article by Peter Hughes, 'Vico and Literary History,' *Yale Italian Studies* 1 (Winter 1977): 83–90, esp. 85–6.

17 See the preface to the paperback edition of *Fearful Symmetry* (Boston:

Beacon, 1962), in which Frye confesses to ten years of work and five complete rewritings. On the importance of *Fearful Symmetry* to Blake studies, see G.E. Bentley, Jr. and Martin K. Nurmi, *A Blake Bibliography: Annotated Lists of Works, Studies, and Blakeana* (Minneapolis: U of Minnesota P, 1964) 25–6, 269; and G.E. Bentley, Jr., 'Blake on Frye and Frye on Blake,' *The Legacy of Northrop Frye* 177–89. For a somewhat dissenting opinion see Domenico Pietropaolo, 'Frye, Blake, e la boria dei dotti' 135.

18 On the English eighteenth-century sublime, see Samuel Monk, *The Sublime: A Study of Critical Theories in XVIII-Century England* (Ann Arbor: U of Michigan P, 1960); and D.B. Morris, *The Religious Sublime: Christian Poetry and Critical Tradition in 18th-Century England* (Lexington, KY: UP of Kent, 1972). For a broad survey of contemporary critical work on the sublime, see Gustavo Costa, 'Considerazioni inattuali sul sublime,' *Forum Italicum* 23.1–2 (Spring–Fall 1989): 80–104.

19 This article was later included in a collection of Frye's early reviews under the new title 'The Rhythm of Growth and Decay,' *Northrop Frye on Culture and Literature: A Collection of Review Essays*, ed. Robert D. Denham (Chicago: U of Chicago P, 1978) 141–6.

20 Note the early references to Cassirer in the article 'The Archetypes of Literature,' first published in the *Kenyon Review* 13 (Winter 1951): 92–110, and later incorporated into the Second Essay of *Anatomy of Criticism* and rpt. in *Fables of Identity* 7–20. See also 'Art in a New Modulation' (a review of Susanne K. Langer's *Feeling and Form*), *Hudson Review* 6 (Summer 1953): 313–17, rpt. in *Northrop Frye on Culture and Literature* 111–16; and 'Myth as Information' (a review of Ernst Cassirer's *Philosophy of Symbolic Forms*, vol. 1), *Hudson Review* 7 (Summer 1954): 228–35, also rpt. in *Northrop Frye on Culture and Literature* 67–75. It is very unlikely that Frye was unaware of Samuel Beckett's discussion of the Vichian elements in Joyce, published in the essay entitled 'Dante ... Bruno. Vico ... Joyce' in *Our Exagmination Round His Factification for Incamination of Work in Progress* (1929; London: Faber and Faber, 1961), and of Benedetto Croce's important re-interpretation of Vico contained in *The Philosophy of Giambattista Vico*, published in R.G. Collingwood's English translation in 1913.

21 For commentaries on this specific acknowledgment of Vico's influence by Frye, see Domenico Pietropaolo, 'Frye, Vico, and the Grounding of Literature and Criticism' 95–6, and Ian Balfour, *Northrop Frye* 69.

22 For some early considerations of Vico's relation to Frye, see Angus Fletcher, 'Utopian History and the *Anatomy of Criticism*,' *Northrop Frye in Modern Criticism*, ed. Murray Krieger (New York: Columbia UP, 1966) 31–73; Timothy Bahti, 'Vico and Frye: A Note,' *New Vico Studies* 3 (1985): 119–29; and

Peter Hughes, 'Vico and Literary History,' *Yale Italian Studies* 1 (Winter 1977): 83–90.

Chapter 1   Process, the Sublime, and the Eighteenth Century

1 See Joseph Addison, 'Pleasures of the Imagination,' *Selections from the Spectator*, introduction and notes by K. Deighton (London: Macmillan, 1927), esp. nos. 411–12; and John Dennis (1657–1734), *The Grounds of Criticism in Poetry* (1704; New York: Garland Publishing, 1971).

2 Vincent DeLuca, *Words of Eternity: Blake and the Poetics of the Sublime* (New Jersey: Princeton UP, 1991).

3 Authorship of the first-century treatise *On the Sublime* has been traditionally, if erroneously, ascribed to one Longinus, sometimes referred to as 'Pseudo-Longinus' because of the ongoing inconclusiveness surrounding the true identity of the author of this important text.

4 For a discussion of the emergence of the non-normative poetics of possible world theory during this epoch, see Lubomir Doležel, *Occidental Poetics: Tradition and Progress* (Lincoln and London: U of Nebraska P, 1990), esp. ch. 2.

5 It is not surprising to find, then, that, as Domenico Pietropaolo has noted, Plotinus's notion of the mind as *dator formarum* is presupposed in Frye's concept of the human creative intellect. See 'Northrop Frye e la paideia della libertà,' *Belfagor* 4 (1992): 403–18.

6 I do not intend here to suggest any diametrical contrast between Vico and Locke for, while Vico did draw substantially different epistemological conclusions, he was quite receptive to much in Locke. See Gustavo Costa, 'Vico e Locke,' *Giornale critico della filosofia italiana* 4th ser. 1.49 (1970): 344–61. For a commentary that qualifies Vico's anti-Cartesianism see Yvon Beleval, 'Vico and Anti-Cartesianism,' *Giambattista Vico: An International Symposium*, ed. Giorgio Tagliacozzo and Hayden White (Baltimore: Johns Hopkins UP, 1969) 77–91.

7 For a preliminary discussion of Vico, Blake, Frye, and the *verum factum* principle, see Nella Cotrupi, '*Verum Factum*: Viconian Markers along Frye's Path,' *The Legacy of Northrop Frye* 286–95.

8 'The Ideas of Northrop Frye,' pt. 3, CBC Radio documentary written and presented by David Cayley, 5 Mar. 1990, transcribed in the *Northrop Frye Newsletter* (ed. Robert D. Denham) 4.1 (Winter 1991–92): 7–18. See also David Cayley, *Northrop Frye in Conversation* (Concord, Ont.: Anansi, 1992) 5.

9 Ironically, it is the arch-conservative Edmund Burke, whose reputation rests on two treatises – one on the French Revolution and the other on the

sublime – who epitomizes this coincidence of the sublime and the revolu-
tionary. See Edmund Burke, *A Philosophical Enquiry into the Origin of Our
Ideas of the Sublime*, ed. and intro. by J.T. Boulton (London: Routledge and
Kegan Paul, 1958), and Edmund Burke, *Reflections on the French Revolution*
(Indianapolis: Bobbs-Merill, 1955). For a partial consideration of this
conjunction, see Baldine Saint Girons, *Fiat Lux: Une Philosophie du Sublime*
(Paris: Quai Voltaire, 1993), esp. 364–423. See also Tom Furniss, *Edmund
Burke's Aesthetic Ideology: Language, Gender, and Political Economy in Revolution*
(New York: Cambridge UP, 1993).

10 On Frye's Aristotelianism, see, for example, Giles Carrier, 'La critique
est-elle une science?' *Études Françaises* (Montreal) (6 May 1970): 221–6;
A.C. Hamilton, *Northrop Frye: Anatomy of his Criticism* 153; W.K. Wimsatt,
'Northrop Frye: Criticism as Myth,' *Northrop Frye in Modern Criticism* 75–107.
For a divergent opinion, see Robert D. Denham, *Northrop Frye and Critical
Method* 29–30.

11 For a preliminary exploration of Frye and the sublime, see Nella Cotrupi,
'Vico, Burke and Frye's Flirtation with the Sublime,' *Giambattista Vico and
Anglo-American Science, Philosophy, and Writing* (Berlin: Mouton de Gruyter,
1995) 35–49.

12 For a more general discussion of Aristotle's concept of catharsis and a brief
discussion of Frye on catharsis, see Francis Sparshott, 'The Riddle of
Katharsis,' *Centre and Labyrinth* 14–37.

13 Francis Sparshott, 'The Riddle of *Katharsis*' 18.

14 For an extended application of the product/process distinction in the
context of metafictional works, see Linda Hutcheon, *Narcissistic Narrative*
(New York: Methuen, 1980), esp. ch. 2.

15 Howard D. Weinbrot has challenged Frye on this aspect of the 'age of
sensibility,' saying, 'Frye's anorexic "process" cannot be nourished by the
ample feast of eighteenth-century literature, its affective aesthetics, and its
familiar dialogue between creating author and creating audience ... a
putative exemplar like Sterne subverts process, and ... a putative adversary
like Fielding often embodies process.' 'Northrop Frye and the Literature of
Process Reconsidered,' *Eighteenth-Century Studies* 24.2 (Winter 1990–91):
173–95.

16 For a detailed discussion of Vico's response to Longinus in the context of
his commentary on Dante, see Domenico Pietropaolo, *Dante Studies in the
Age of Vico* (Ottawa: Dovehouse, 1989), esp. 81–92.

17 For a concise history of scholarship on the sublime since its revival, see
Gustavo Costa, 'Considerazioni inattuali sul sublime,' *Forum Italicum* 23.1–2
(Spring–Fall 1989): 80–104.

18 For a discussion of the impact of Edmund Burke and the English discourse on the sublime on Kant, see Luigi Russo, introduction to *Da Longino a Longino: I luoghi del Sublime*, ed. Luigi Russo (Palermo: Aesthetica, 1987) 7–16.

19 The profound link between sublimity and postmodernity has been the subject of considerable scrutiny in Jean-François Lyotard, *The Postmodern Condition*.

20 See John Dennis, *The Grounds of Criticism in Poetry*; Joseph Addison, 'Pleasures of the Imagination,' *Selections from the Spectator*; and Robert Lowth, *Lectures on the Sacred Poetry of the Hebrews*, trans. G. Gregory (New York: Garland Publishing, 1971).

Chapter 2   Against a Separate Nature

1 See especially Daniel O'Hara, *The Romance of Interpretation: Visionary Criticism from Pater to de Man* (New York: Columbia UP, 1985), and Gerald Graff, *Literature Against Itself* (Chicago: U of Chicago P, 1979).

2 I substitute the word 'poetics' for 'aesthetics' here because Frye's critical focus is primarily aimed at the properties, processes, and functions of language in culture and society, and not at artefacts in general.

3 See J.T. Boulton, introduction to Edmund Burke, *A Philosophical Enquiry into the Origin of our Ideas of the Sublime and Beautiful* (London: Routledge and Kegan Paul, 1958) cxxv–cxxvii.

4 For an extended discussion of the gendering of the categories of the beautiful and the sublime in Burke's *Enquiry*, see Frances Ferguson, 'The Sublime of Edmund Burke: the Bathos of Experience,' *Glyph* 8 (1981): 62–78. See also Terry Eagleton, *The Ideology of the Aesthetic* 54; and Samuel H. Monk, *The Sublime* (Ann Arbor: U of Michigan P, 1935) 67.

5 A.C. Hamilton, in *Northrop Frye: Anatomy of his Criticism*, similarly observes that 'For Frye ... literature seeks to transform nature instead of annihilating it, the goal being a rehabilitated nature' (274n16). He then refers the reader to 'An Interview with Northrop Frye,' *Scripsi* (University of Melbourne) 2.4 (1984): 222; and A.C. Hamilton, 'Northrop Frye: The Visionary Critic,' *CEA Critic* 42 (November 1979): 2–6.

Chapter 3   Vico and the Making of Truth

1 In other publications Pietropaolo has focused to a greater extent on the prophetic or process aspect of Frye's critical thinking. See especially 'Northrop Frye,' *I discorsi della critica in America*, ed. John Picchione (Roma: Bulzoni, 1993) 23–37.

2 In *The Critical Path*, Frye writes: 'The conventions, genres and archetypes of
   literature do not simply appear: they must develop historically from origins
   or perhaps from a common origin. In pursuing this line of thought, I have
   turned repeatedly to Vico, one of the very few thinkers to understand
   anything of the historical role of the poetic impulse in civilization as a
   whole' (39). For commentary on this description of Vico as guide, see Ian
   Balfour, *Northrop Frye* 69, and Domenico Pietropaolo, 'Frye, Vico, and the
   Grounding of Literature and Criticism' 95–6.

3 See especially Gustavo Costa, 'Considerazioni inattuali sul sublime,' *Forum
   Italicum* 23.1–2 (Spring–Fall 1989): 80–104. Also of interest on Vico and the
   Longinian tradition are Gustavo Costa, 'Vico and Ancient Rhetoric,' *Classi-
   cal Influences on Western Thought, A.D. 1650–1870*, ed. R.R. Bolgar (New York
   and London: Cambridge UP, 1979) 247–62; and 'G.B. Vico e lo pseudo-
   Longino,' *Giornale critico della filosofia italiana* 47 (1968): 502–28.

4 'Forse Vico è stato il primo ad intuire quanto stava accadendo nella estrema
   frase di trapasso dalla mentalità prescientifica a quella scientifica, se si
   pensa alla sua rivendicazione della dimensione mitica e magica,
   inscindibile dalla poesia sublime' (86).

5 'L'Occidente è diventato romantico, riconoscendosi nella idea della
   immaginazione creatrice, che attribuisce all'artista un potere analogo a
   quello di Dio, creatore del mondo *ex nihilo*. Questa concezione, estranea
   allo spirito greco, poteva conciliarsi meglio con il vago misticismo dello
   Pseudo-Longino che con Aristotele, e pertanto la critica occidentale è
   diventata longiniana. Ancora oggi il travaglio critico si attua fra i poli
   segnati da Aristotele e dallo Pseudo-Longino, se Northrop Frye ha potuto
   additare una concezione letteraria di stampo longiniano, tematica e
   creativa, fondata sulla estasi, per contrapporla ad una concezione letteraria
   di stampo aristotelico, estetica e distaccata fondata sulla catarsi' (91).

6 For an overview of process theology and of its links to Whitehead's thought,
   see Robert B. Mellert, *What is Process Theology?* (New York: Paulist P, 1975).
   See also *Religious Experience and Process Theology*, ed. Henry James Cargas and
   Bernard Lee (New York: Paulist P, 1976); and *Process Theology and Christian
   Thought*, ed. Delwin Brown, Ralph E. James, Jr., and Gene Reeves (New
   York: Bobbs-Merrill, 1971).

7 To date the influence of Whitehead on Frye does not seem to have gar-
   nered a great deal of attention. A.C. Hamilton makes a passing reference to
   the 'fallacy of misplaced concreteness' and to *Science and the Modern World*
   in *Northrop Frye: Anatomy of his Criticism* 78. Whitehead is not listed in the
   name and subject index of Robert D. Denham's *Annotated Bibliography*. See,
   however, Craig Stewart Walker, 'Religious Experience in the Work of
   Northrop Frye,' *The Legacy of Northrop Frye* 41; Robert D. Denham, 'Inter-

penetration as a Key Concept in Frye's Critical Vision,' *Rereading Frye* 140–63; and Nella Cotrupi, 'Frye and Whitehead: Interpenetration and Process,' unpublished paper delivered 19 May 2000 at the conference 'Frye and the Word' at McMaster University, Hamilton, Ontario.

8 For a contrasting assessment of the accommodation reached between Vico's humanism and his Catholic faith, see John Milbank, *The Religious Dimension in the Thought of Giambattista Vico, 1668–1744* (Queenston, ON: Edwin Mellen P, 1991).

9 See especially pages 99–142 for Berlin's discussion of Vico's *verum factum*. Among earlier works on this topic, see especially Benedetto Croce, *The Philosophy of Giambattista Vico* (1911). See also Isaiah Berlin, 'A Note on Vico's Concept of Knowledge,' *Giambattista Vico: An International Symposium*, ed. Giorgio Tagliacozzo and Hayden White, 371–7.

10 This is not to suggest that Vico did not benefit from other aspects of Locke's thought. Gustavo Costa sees Vico's primitivistic conception of poetry to be founded on two key elements, 'the Longinian sublime and Locke's epoch-making contribution to the history of psychology,' in the essay 'Vico and Ancient Rhetoric' 257. For a more detailed discussion of Costa's understanding of Locke's impact on Vico, see Gustavo Costa, 'Vico e Locke,' *Giornale critico della filosofia italiana* 4th ser. 1.49 (1970): 344–61; id. 'Vico e il Settecento,' *Forum Italicum* 10 (1976): 10–30.

11 See, for example, chapters 1 and 35 of *On the Sublime*.

12 'Vico and Ancient Rhetoric' 255n3. See also Isaiah Berlin's discussion of the Vico-Burke connection in *Vico and Herder* 72.

13 Frances Ferguson, 'The Sublime of Edmund Burke' 69.

14 On the importance of the body in Vico's thought, see Giuseppe Modica, 'Umanesimo e corporietà in Vico,' *Giambattista Vico: Poesia, logica, religione* (Brescia: Marceliana, 1986) 352–66; and Gianfranco Cantelli, *Mente, corpo, linguaggio: saggio sull'interpretazione vichiana del mito* (Firenze: Sansone, 1986).

15 'Dunque, chi s'avvia non già alla fisica e alla meccanica, bensì alle cariche publiche o alla vita forense o alle discussioni delle assemblee ovvero alla predicazione, non s'indugi, né da fanciullo né a lungo, in questi insegnamenti condotti secondo il metodo cartesiano. Per contrario, studi, attraverso le figure e con un metodo ingegnoso, la geometria; cultivi la topica, e, con tono spigliato ed elegante, discetti, in un senso e in quello opposto, sulla natura, sull'uomo, sullo Stato, per imparare ad abbracciare quanto nelle cose v'ha di più probabile e più verisimile. E ciò, perché noi moderni dobbiam mirare non già a divenire più colti, nell'insieme, degli antichi e lasciare che questi restino più saggi di noi; non già a divenire più degli antichi aderenti al vero e lasciare che questi restino più eloquenti di

noi; ma ad esser pari agli antichi nella saggezza e nell'eloquenza, così come
li superiamo nella scienza' (*Metodo degli studi, Opere* 201). The English
translation is from *On the Study Methods of Our Time*, trans. Elio Gianturco
(New York: Bobbs-Merrill, 1965) 41. (All subsequent translations of this text
are from this edition.)

16 For a discussion of the philosophical issues in this oration, see Ernesto
Grassi, 'Critical Philosophy or Topical Philosophy? Meditations on the *De
nostri temporis studiorum ratione*,' *Giambattista Vico: An International Symposium*
39–50.

17 'Pertanto ti avvedrai che tutti i fisici moderni s'avvalgono d'una forma
letteraria laconica e austera; e poiché codesta sorta di fisica, sia quando la si
impari, sia quando la si insegni, non attende perpetuamente ad altro che a
fare scaturire una proposizione da quella che immediatamente la precede,
essa ottunde negli ascoltatori quella facoltà, che, peculiare ai filosofi,
consiste nello scorgere simiglianze ideali in cose quanto mai lontane e
diverse, ch'è come dire quella ch'è reputata fonte precipua di qualunque
forma letteraria acuta e ornata. E invero dir "sottile" non è lo stesso che
dire 'acuto': il sottile consta di una linea sola, l'acuto di due. Tra i detti
acuti il posto preeminente spetta alla metafora, che, più di ogni altra cosa,
è splendore insigne e ornamento luculentissimo di qualunque parlare
ornato' (*Opere* 184–5).

18 'Alla prudenza civile importa, nelle azioni umane, scorgere il vero quale
esso è, e sia pure un vero originato da mancanza di senno, da ignoranza, da
capriccio, da necessità, da fortuna: la poesia, invece, mira esclusivamente al
vero quale dovrebbe essere per natura e razionalità' (Opere 203–4).

19 '[il poeta] s'allontana da ciò che nella natura é incerto per seguire ciò che
in essa è costante; s'attiene, dunque, al falso per essere, in certo qual modo,
più veritiero' (*Opere* 203).

20 I rely here on the Italian translation by Fausto Nicolini, entitled
Dell'Antichissima Sapienza Italica, Giambattista Vico, *Opere* 243–308; and on
the English translation by L.M. Palmer (Ithaca, NY: Cornell UP, 1988).

21 In his letter to Gherardo degli Angioli, Vico bemoans the fact that degli
Angioli was born in an epoch rendered too subtle by analytical thinking, by
a philosophy that stifles those faculties of the human being that are rooted
in the body (*Opere* 121–6).

22 *On the Most Ancient Wisdom of the Italians*, trans. L.M. Palmer (Ithaca, NY:
Cornell UP, 1988) 97. All English translations of this oration quoted in the
text are taken from this translation.

23 'Il conoscere distinguendo, come quello che è un conoscere i confini delle
cose, è più un difetto che non un pregio della mente umana. La mente

divina le vede nel sole della verità; il che vuol dire che, nel vederne una, ne
conosce, insieme con questa, infinite altre: tutt'al contrario della mente
umana, che, nel conoscere una cosa distinguendola, la vede al lume
notturno d'una lucerna; il che significa che, vedendola, perde, nella
visione di essa, quella delle circostanti' (*Opere* 277).

24 On Vico's theory of metaphor, see also John D. Schaeffer, 'From Wit to
Narration: Vico's Theory of Metaphor in its Rhetorical Context,' *New Vico
Studies* 2 (1984): 59–73; Donatella Di Cesare, 'Sul concetto di metafora in
G.B. Vico,' Bollettino del Centro di Studi Vichiani 16 (1986): 325–34; and
Gillo Dorfles, 'Myth and Metaphor in Vico and in Contemporary Aesthet-
ics,' *Giambattista Vico: An International Symposium* 577–90.

25 Quotations in the original Italian are from the edition of 1744 included in
Giambattista Vico, *Opere*, ed. Fausto Nicolini. English translations are taken
from Giambattista Vico, *The New Science*, abridged trans. of the 1744 edition,
by Thomas Goddard Bergin and Max Harold Fisch (Ithaca, NY: Cornell UP,
1948, 1970). Parenthetical references are to paragraph, not page, numbers.

26 'È altra proprietà della mente umana ch'ove gli uomini delle cose lontane e
non conosciute non possono fare niuna idea, le stimano dalle cose loro
conosciute e presenti.

Questa degnità addita il fonte inesausto di tutti gli errori presi
dall'intiere nazioni e da tutt'i dotti d'intorno a'princìpi dell'umanità;
perocché da'loro tempi illuminati, colti e magnifici, ne'quali cominciarono
quelle ad avvertirle, questi a ragionarle, hanno estimato l'origine
dell'umanità, le quali dovettero per natura essere picciole, rozze,
oscurissime' (*Scienza nuova* 122–3, *Opere* 435).

27 'Ma, in tal densa notte di tenebre ond'è coverta la prima da noi
lontanissima antichità, apparisce questo lume eterno, che non tramonta, di
questa verità, la quale non si può a patto alcuno chiamar in dubbio: che
questo mondo civile egli certamente è stato fatto dagli uomini, onde
se ne possono, perché se ne debbono, ritruovare i princìpi dentro le
modificazioni della nostra medesima mente umana. Lo che, a chiunque vi
rifletta, dee recar maraviglia come tutti i filosofi seriosamente si studiarono
di conseguire la scienza di questo mondo naturale, del quale, perché Iddio
egli il fece, esso solo ne ha la scienza; e trascurarono di meditare su questo
mondo delle nazioni, o sia mondo civile, del quale, perché l'avevano fatto
gli uomini, ne potevano conseguire la scienza gli uomini. Il quale
stravagante effetto è provenuto da quella miseria, la qual avvertimmo nelle
Degnità della mente umana, la quale, restata immersa e seppellita nel
corpo, è naturalmente inchinata a sentire le cose del corpo e dee usare
troppo sforzo e fatica per intendere se medesima, come l'occhio corporale

che vede tutti gli obbietti fuori di sé ed ha dello specchio bisogno per vedere se stesso' (*Scienza nuova* 331, *Opere* 479–80).

28 On Vico's imaginative universals, see also Donald Phillip Verene, 'Vico's Science of Imaginative Universals and the Philosophy of Symbolic Forms,' *Giambattista Vico's Science of Humanity*, ed. Giorgio Tagliacozzo and Donald Phillip Verene (Baltimore: Johns Hopkins UP, 1976) 295–317.

29 For a discussion of Vico's model of history and its reliance on tropes, see Hayden White, *Metahistory* (Baltimore: Johns Hopkins UP, 1973), esp. 230–3; see also Hayden White, 'The Tropics of History: The Deep Structure of the *New Science,*' *Giambattista Vico's Science of Humanity* 65–85.

30 For a preliminary account see Frank Nuessel, 'Metaphor and Cognition: A Review Essay,' *Metaphor, Communication and Cognition*, ed. Marcel Danesi, Toronto Semiotic Circle, monograph series 2 (1987–88): 87–98. For a detailed discussion of Vico's theories of the origin of language in the context of present-day research, see Marcel Danesi, *Vico, Metaphor, and the Origin of Language* (Bloomington: Indiana UP, 1993).

Chapter 4   Process and Freedom

1 See especially Benedetto Croce, *La filosofia di G.B. Vico*, first published in 1911 and translated into English by R.G. Collingwood in 1913.

2 Frye writes in the essay of 1983 entitled 'Blake's Biblical Illustrations' that 'Blake had not read Vico, but he had developed parallel intuitions from contemporary books,' Northrop Frye, *The Eternal Act of Creation* (Bloomington: Indiana UP, 1993) 66. Also in the same text, Frye writes: 'For Blake there was a more important distinction between the passive attitude that stares at the world and the active or creative one that builds something out of it. The former is what Blake calls "reason" and regards as stupid; the latter, its direct opposite, he calls mental, intellectual or imaginative' (64). For a longer meditation by Frye on the links between Blake's thought and Vico's *verum factum* principle, see 'Blake's Bible,' *Myth and Metaphor* (Charlottesville, VA: UP of Virginia 1990), esp. 285–6. In commenting on Frye's links to Ernst Cassirer, A.C. Hamilton notes that both accept Vico's *verum factum* principle and that 'Frye would be open to Cassirer's influence because Blake had taught him that "art ... transforms nature into a home" (*FS* 265),' *Northrop Frye* 249n37.

3 Robert D. Denham pointed out very early that Frye explicitly acknowledges his debt to Oswald Spengler insofar as the theory of modes in *Anatomy* is concerned. But as Frye also states, it was Vico who confirmed his own preference for the notion of aging and renewal over that of decline found

in Spengler. See Robert D. Denham, *Northrop Frye and Critical Method* 14–15, 235n12. See also Northrop Frye, *Spiritus Mundi* (Bloomington: Indiana UP, 1976) 113, and Northrop Frye, *The Critical Path* (Bloomington: Indiana UP, 1971) 34.

4 For a discussion of the implications of this modal approach to criticism in the context of intercultural dialogue, see Eva Kushner, 'Northrop Frye et la possibilité du dialogue interculturel,' *Recherches Sémiotiques/Semiotic Inquiry* 13.3 (1993): 23–31.

5 *I and Thou*, trans. R.G. Smith (1953; Edinburgh: T. and T. Clark, 1958).

6 For a succinct discussion of Vico's privileging of mythic or fabular figuration as a precursor for philosophical thought and the implications of such as position, see Stephen H. Daniel, 'Vico on Mythic Figuration as Prerequisite for Philosophic Literacy,' *New Vico Studies* 3 (1985): 61–71.

7 Jonathan Hart has noted that Frye's emphasis on the function of literature in seeking the possible in the actual is in keeping with possible worlds theory; this is particularly suggestive if one considers that Vico's *verum factum* principle, which sustains much of Frye's thought on this point, has been linked to possible worlds theory. This connection deserves much more thorough exploration, particularly given the contributions to possible worlds theory of Vico's near contemporary, Leibniz. See Jonathan Hart, 'Frye's Anatomizing and Anatomizing Frye,' *Canadian Review of Comparative Literature* 19.1–2 (Mar/June 1992): 119–54; and on Vico and possible worlds, see Horst Steinke, 'Hintikka and Vico: An Update on Contemporary Logic,' *New Vico Studies* 3 (1985): 147–55. For a discussion of Leibniz and possible worlds see Lubomir Doležel, *Occidental Poetics: Tradition and Progress*; esp. 33–52.

Chapter 5   Process, Concern, and Interpenetration

1 For a more extended discussion of *kerygma* in Frye see Alvin A. Lee, 'Northrop Frye: Identity not Negation,' *Recherches Sémiotiques/Semiotic Inquiry* 13.3 (1993): 33–46.

2 In an essay entitled 'Frye and Ideology,' first delivered at the conference on 'The Legacy of Northrop Frye' held in October 1992 at the University of Toronto, Imre Salusinszky rejects Frye's attempt to distinguish mythology and ideology on the basis of primary and secondary concerns and arrives at the following observation: 'Unfortunately, though, all of this belief in some "primary" terrain sounds exactly like an ideology itself. Indeed, such an invocation of a realm of "natural" or "primary" human needs, transcending all distinctions of race, class, and gender, and connected with the aesthetic,

is precisely what contemporary left cultural critics mean when they talk about an "aesthetic ideology." By defining, as it were, the minimum of what is essential for all human beings you can end up producing a highly distilled version of the Western liberal ideology itself.' See *The Legacy of Northrop Frye* 78–9. For a different analysis of ideology and mythology in Frye's thinking, see Jonathan Hart, *Northrop Frye: The Theoretical Imagination* (London: Routledge, 1994) 191–242; and Joseph Adamson, 'The Treason of the Clerks: Frye, Ideology, and the Authority of Imaginative Culture,' *Rereading Frye* 72–102.

3 Nella Cotrupi, unpublished manuscript entitled 'The Meaning of Myth in Roland Barthes and Northrop Frye,' delivered 31 March 1994 at the University of Toronto.

4 For a discussion of the role of memory in Vico, see esp. Donald Phillip Verene, 'The New Art of Narration: Vico and the Muses,' *New Vico Studies* 1 (1983): 23; and *Vico's Science of Imagination* (Ithaca, NY: Cornell UP, 1981), esp. 69–126. Frye aknowledged this aspect of Vico's work in Notebook 19, par. 343, where he writes, 'A much vaguer synthesis, also suggested by Vico, takes shape in the background, of an encyclopaedic spatialization of knowledge. The bases for this are Curtius' study of topoi, particularly their literal sense as "places," the book of Frances Yates on the arts of memory and the idea of the cave-theatre holding all the ghosts of imagination like the one in PU [*Prometheus Unbound*].' For a discussion of memory, see Imre Salusinszky, 'Frye and the Art of Memory,' *Rereading Frye* 39–54.

5 For an earlier published version of these ideas, see *Creation and Recreation* 70; or *Northrop Frye on Religion* (Toronto: U of Toronto P, 2000) 79.

6 Robert D. Denham, 'Interpenetration as a Key Concept in Frye's Critical Vision,' *Rereading Frye* 140–63.

7 On Teilhard de Chardin as process thinker, see Dan G. Barbour, 'Teilhard's Process Metaphysics,' *The Journal of Religions* 49.2 (April 1964): 136–59; and Kenneth Conthan, *Science, Secularization and God* (Nashville: Abingdon P, 1969).

8 See, for example, Notes 53, par. 97, *Northrop Frye's Late Notebooks, 1982–1990: Architecture of the Spiritual World*, ed. Robert D. Denham (Toronto: U of Toronto P, 2000) 2:631 and NB 34, par. 69, Northrop Frye Fonds, 1991, box 26, Victoria University Library.

9 See Robert D. Denham, 'Interpenetration as a Key Concept in Frye's Critical Vision,' *Rereading Frye* 140–63; and Margaret Burgess, 'The Resistance to Religion: Anxieties Surrounding the Spiritual Dimensions of Frye's Thought; or, Investigations into the Fear of Enlightenment,' *The Legacy of Northrop Frye* 59–75.

10 I owe this usage of the word 'abyss' to the philosopher Ernesto Grassi, who enunciates the importance of the experience of radical metaphor to the sublime even more explicitly than does Northrop Frye. See especially 'Il sublime e l'esperienza della parola,' *Da Longino a Longino: I luoghi del Sublime* 161–76.

11 See Rudolph Bultmann, *Theology of the New Testament*, vol. 1, trans. Kendrick Grobel (New York: Scribner's, 1951) 3–53. See also Hans Werner Bartsch, *Kerygma and Myth: A Theological Debate*, trans. Reginald H. Fuller (London: SPCK, 1954).

Conclusion: The Ethics and *Praxis* of Process

1 For a general discussion of Vico and education, see Maria Goretti, 'Vico's Pedagogic Thought and that of Today,' *Giambattista Vico: An International Symposium* 553–76. Goretti notes that the bibliography on Vico as educator is limited, particularly in the non-Italian world. See also R. Fornaca, *Il pensiero educativo di Giambattista Vico* (Turin: Giappichelli, 1957). For an interesting American perspective on Vico and autodidacticism, see Edward Said, *Beginnings: Intention and Method* (New York: Basic Books, 1975) 358–66; and 'Vico: Autodidact and Humanist,' *The Centennial Review of Arts and Science* 11 (1967): 336–52.

2 This text contains the English translations by Giorgio A. Pinton and Arthur W. Shippee of six of Vico's inaugural orations, delivered at the University of Naples during the first part of the eighteenth century.

3 Also called at times 'Giudizio sopra Dante.' As Domenico Pietropaolo has discussed, this title, which was given to the oration by Fausto Nicolini, is somewhat misleading because of the date of this essay's composition. See Domenico Pietropaolo, *Dante Studies in the Age of Vico* (Ottawa: Dovehouse, 1989) 102n25.

4 See especially chapters 2 and 6 of *Contingencies of Value: Alternative Perspectives for Critical Theory* (Cambridge, MA: Harvard UP, 1988).

5 For a comprehensive account of how Vico's *verum factum* principle constitutes an ethical anti-foundational alternative to scepticism, and thus posits a more constructive version of modernity, see John Milbank, *The Religious Dimension of the Thought of Giambattista Vico, 1668–1744*, Studies in the History of Philosophy, vol. 23 (Lewiston, ON: Edwin Mellen Press, 1991).

6 See especially 'Northrop Frye: Parameters of Mythological Structuralism,' *Telos* 27 (Spring 1976): 40–60; and 'Northrop Frye: A Critical Theory of Capitulation,' *The Critical Twilight: Explorations in Ideology of Anglo-American Literary Theory from Eliot to McLuhan* 107–31.

7 Hayden White had by this time already published extensively on the question of Frye's Vichian brand of modal criticism and its applicability to all
narratives, including those of an historical variety, but Fekete makes no
reference to this. See Hayden White, *Metahistory: The Historical Imagination
in Nineteenth-Century Europe* (Baltimore: Johns Hopkins UP, 1973), esp.
7–11, 231–3; see also 'The Structure of Historical Narrative,' *Clio* 1 (June
1972): 5–20.

8 For a brief assessment of Frye's international reputation, see Robert D.
Denham, 'Auguries of Influence,' *Visionary Poetics* 77–92.

9 The term 'epistemological asymmetry' is used by Barbara Herrnstein Smith
in, for example, *Contingencies of Value* 173; and 'The Unquiet Judge: Activism without Objectivism in Law and Politics,' *Rethinking Objectivity*, Annals of
Scholarship, double issue, ed. Allan Megill, 1992.

10 See, for example, John Fekete, *The Critical Twilight* 110.

Works Cited

Abrams, M.H. *The Mirror and the Lamp: Romantic Theory and the Critical Tradition.* New York: Oxford UP, 1953.

Adams, Hazard. 'Essay on Frye.' *Visionary Poetics: Essays on Northrop Frye's Criticism.* Ed. Robert D. Denham and Thomas Willard. New York: Peter Lang, 1991. 41–56.

Adamson, Joseph. *Northrop Frye: A Visionary Life.* Toronto: ECW P, 1993.

Addison, Joseph. 'Pleasures of the Imagination.' *Selections from the Spectator.* Intro. and notes by K. Deighton. London: Macmillan, 1927.

Adorno, Theodor W. *Aesthetic Theory.* London: Routledge and Kegan Paul, 1984.

Albrecht, William Price. *The Sublime Pleasures of Tragedy: A Study of Critical Theory from Dennis to Keats.* Lawrence: UP of Kansas, 1975.

Aristotle. *Poetics. Introduction to Aristotle.* Ed. Richard McKeon. 2nd ed. Chicago: U of Chicago P, 1973. 662–713.

Ayre, John. *Northrop Frye: A Biography.* Toronto: Random House, 1989.

Bahti, Timothy. 'Vico and Frye: A Note.' *New Vico Studies* 3 (1985): 119–29.

Balfour, Ian. 'Can the Centre Hold? Northrop Frye and the Spirit of the World.' *Essays in Canadian Writing* 7/8 (Fall 1977): 214–21.

– *Northrop Frye.* Boston: G.K. Hall, 1988.

Bartsch, Hans Werner. *Kerygma and Myth: A Theological Debate.* Trans. Reginald H. Fuller. London: SPCK P, 1945.

Beckett, Samuel. 'Dante ... Bruno. Vico ... Joyce.' *Our Exagmination Round His Factification for Incamination of Work in Progress.* 1929. London: Faber and Faber, 1961.

Beleval, Yvon. 'Vico and Anti-Cartesianism.' Tagliacozo and White 77–91.

Bentley, Jr., G.E. and Martin K. Nurmi. *A Blake Bibliography: Annotated Lists of Works, Studies, and Blakeana.* Minneapolis: U of Minnesota P, 1964.

Berlin, Isaiah. *Vico and Herder: Two Studies in the History of Ideas.* New York: Viking, 1976.

– 'A Note on Vico's Concept of Knowledge.' Tagliacozzo and White 371–7.

Blumenberg, Hans. *Work on Myth.* Cambridge, MA: MIT P, 1985.

Booth, Wayne. Critical Understanding: The Powers and Limits of Pluralism. Chicago: U of Chicago P, 1979.

– *The Rhetoric of Irony.* Chicago: U of Chicago P, 1974.

Bourdieu, Pierre, and Alain Darbel. *La Distinction: Critique social du jugement.* Paris: Les Éditions de Minuit, 1979.

Boyd, David, and Imre Salusinszky, eds. *Rereading Frye: The Published and Unpublished Works.* Toronto: U of Toronto P, 1999.

Brody, Jules. *Boileau and Longinus.* Geneva: E. Droz, 1958.

Buber, Martin. *I and Thou.* 1953. Trans. R.G. Smith. Edinburgh: T and T Clark, 1958.

Bultmann, Rudolph. *Theology of the New Testament.* Vol. 1. Trans. Kendrick Grobel. New York: Scribner's, 1951.

Burke, Edmund. *A Philosophical Enquiry into the Origin of our Ideas of the Sublime and the Beautiful.* Ed. and intro. J.T. Boulton. London: Routledge and Kegan Paul, 1958.

Cantelli, Gianfranco. *Mente, corpo, linguaggio: saggio sull'interpretazione vichiana del mito.* Firenze: Sansone, 1986.

Carrier, Giles. 'La critique est-elle une science?' *Études Françaises* [Montreal] 6 (May 1970): 221–6.

Cayley, David. *Northrop Frye in Conversation.* Concord, ON: Anansi, 1992.

– 'The Ideas of Northrop Frye.' Pts. 1–3. CBC Radio Documentary. 19, 25 Feb. and 5 Mar. 1990. Rpt. in *Northrop Frye Newsletter.* Ed. Robert D. Denham. 3.1 (Winter 1990–91): 2–14; 3.2 (Spring 1991): 2–16; 4.1 (Winter 1991–2): 7–18.

Cook, David. *Northrop Frye: A Vision of the New World.* Montreal: New World Perspectives, 1985.

Costa, Gustavo. 'Considerazioni inattuali sul sublime.' *Forum Italicum* 23.1–2 (Spring–Fall 1989): 80–104.

– 'Vico and Locke.' *Giornale critico della filosofia italiana* 4th ser. 1.49 (1970): 344–61.

– 'G.B. Vico e lo pseudo-Longino.' *Giornale critico della filosofia italiana* 47 (1968): 502–28.

– 'Vico and Ancient Rhetoric.' *Classical Influences on Western Thought,* A.D. *1650–1870.* Ed. R.R. Bolgar. New York: Cambridge UP, 1979. 247–62.

Cotrupi, Nella. '*Verum Factum:* Viconian Markers along Frye's Path.' *The Legacy of Northrop Frye.* Toronto: U of Toronto P, 1994. 286–95.

Croce, Benedetto. *The Philosophy of Giambattista Vico.* 1911. Trans. R.G. Collingwood. London: Latimer, 1913.

Danesi, Marcel. *Vico, Metaphor and the Origin of Language.* Bloomington: Indiana UP, 1993.

— 'Language and the Origin of Human Imagination: A Vichian Perspective.' *New Vico Studies* 4 (1986): 45–56.

Daniel, Stephen H. 'Vico on Mythic Figuration as Prerequisite for Philosophical Literacy.' *New Vico Studies* 3 (1985): 61–71.

de Man, Paul. *Blindness and Insight: Essays in the Rhetoric of Contemporary Criticism.* New York: Oxford UP, 1971.

Denham, Robert D. 'An Anatomy of Frye's Influence.' *American Review of Canadian Studies* 14 (1984): 1–19.

— 'Auguries of Influence.' *Visionary Poetics: Essays on Northrop Frye's Criticism.* Ed. Robert D. Denham and Thomas Willard. New York: Peter Lang, 1991. 77–99.

— *Northrop Frye: An Annotated Bibliography of Primary and Secondary Sources.* Toronto: U of Toronto P, 1990.

— *Northrop Frye and Critical Method.* University Park: Pennsylvania State UP, 1978.

Dennis, John. *The Grounds of Criticism in Poetry.* 1704. New York: Gorland, 1971.

Derrida, Jacques. *The Truth in Painting.* Trans. Geoff Bennington and Ian McLeod. Chicago: U of Chicago P, 1987.

Di Cesare, Donatella. 'Sul concetto di metafora in G.B. Vico.' *Bollettino del Centro di Studi Vichiani* 16 (1986): 325–34.

Doležel, Lubomir. *Occidental Poetics: Tradition and Progress.* Lincoln: U of Nebraska P, 1990.

Donoghue, Denis. 'Mister Myth.' *The New York Review of Books* 9 Apr. 1992: 24–8.

Dorfles, Gillo. 'Myth and Metaphor in Vico and in Contemporary Aesthetics.' Tagliacozzo and White 577–90.

Eagleton, Terry. *The Ideology of the Aesthetic.* Cambridge, MA: Basil Blackwell, 1990.

Eco Umberto. *Semiotics and the Philosophy of Language.* Bloomington: Indiana UP, 1984.

Fekete, John. 'Northrop Frye: A Critical Theory of Capitulation.' *The Critical Twilight: Explorations in Ideology of Anglo-American Literary Theory from Eliot to McLuhan.* London: Routledge and Kegan Paul, 1977. 107–31.

— 'Northrop Frye: Parameters of Mythological Structuralism.' *Telos* 27 (Spring 1976): 40–60.

Ferguson, Frances. *Solitude and the Sublime: Romanticism and the Aesthetics of Individuation.* New York: Routledge, 1992.

– 'The Sublime of Edmund Burke: The Bathos of Experience.' *Glyph* 8 (1981): 62–78.

Fornaca, R. *Il pensiero educativo di Giambattista Vico.* Turin: Giappichelli, 1957.

Fry, Paul H. 'The Possession of the Sublime.' *Studies in Romanticism* 26.2 (Spring 1987): 187–207.

Frye, Northrop. *Anatomy of Criticism: Four Essays.* Princeton: Princeton UP, 1957.

– 'Auguries of Experience.' *Visionary Poetics: Essays on Northrop Frye's Criticism.* Ed. Robert D. Denham and Thomas Willard. New York: Peter Lang, 1991. 1–7.

– *The Correspondence of Northrop Frye and Helen Kemp, 1932–1939.* Ed. Robert D. Denham. 2 vols. Toronto: U of Toronto P, 1996.

– *Creation and Recreation.* Toronto: U of Toronto P, 1980.

– *The Critical Path.* Bloomington: Indiana UP, 1971.

– *Divisions on a Ground: Essays on Canadian Culture.* Ed. James Polk. Toronto: Anansi, 1982.

– *The Double Vision: Language and Meaning in Religion.* Toronto: U of Toronto P, 1991.

– *The Educated Imagination.* The Massey Lectures. 2nd ser. Toronto: CBC, 1963.

– *The Eternal Act of Creation.* Bloomington: Indiana UP, 1993.

– *Fables of Identity: Studies in Poetic Mythology.* New York: Harcourt, Brace and World, 1963.

– *Fearful Symmetry: A Study of William Blake.* 1969 ed. Princeton: Princeton UP, 1947.

– *The Great Code: The Bible and Literature.* Toronto: Academic Press, 1982.

– 'A Letter to the English Institute.' *Northrop Frye in Modern Criticism.* Ed. Murray Krieger. New York: Columbia UP, 1967. 27–30.

– *The Modern Century.* Toronto: Oxford UP, 1967.

– *Myth and Metaphor: Selected Essays, 1974–1988.* Ed. Robert D. Denham. Charlottesville: UP of Virginia, 1990.

– *Northrop Frye on Culture and Literature: A Collection of Review Essays.* Ed. Robert D. Denham. Chicago: U of Chicago P, 1978.

– *Northrop Frye's Student Essays, 1932–1938.* Ed. Robert D. Denham, Toronto: U of Toronto P, 1997.

– *The Secular Scripture: A Study of the Structure of Romance.* Cambridge, MA: Harvard UP, 1976.

– *Spiritus Mundi.* Bloomington: Indiana UP, 1976.

– *The Stubborn Structure: Essays on Criticism and Society.* Ithaca, NY: Cornell UP, 1968.

– *A Study of English Romanticism.* Chicago: U of Chicago P, 1968.
– 'Varieties of Eighteenth-Century Sensibilities.' Ed. Howard D. Weinbrot. *Eighteenth-Century Studies* 24.2 (Winter 1990–91): 157–72.
– *The Well-Tempered Critic.* Markham, ON: Fitzhenry and Whiteside, 1963.
– *Words with Power: Being a Second Study of 'The Bible and Literature.'* Markham, ON: Viking, 1990.
Goretti, Maria. 'Vico's Pedagogic Thought and that of Today.' Tagliacozzo and White 553–76.
Graff, Gerald. *Literature Against Itself.* Chicago: U of Chicago P, 1979.
– 'Northrop Frye and the Visionary Imagination.' *Poetic Statement and Critical Dogma.* Evanstown, IL: Northwestern UP, 1970.
Grassi, Ernesto. 'Critical Philosophy or Topical Philosophy? Meditations on the *De nostri temporis studiorum ratione.*' Tagliacozzo and White 39–50.
– 'Il sublime e l'esperienza della parola.' *Da Longino a Longino: I luoghi del Sublime.* Ed. Luigi Russo. Palermo: Aesthetica, 1987. 161–76.
– *Renaissance Humanism: Studies in Philosophy and Poetics.* Trans. Walter F. Veit. Binghamton, NY: Medieval and Renaissance Texts and Studies, 1988.
Habermas, Jurgen. *The Philosophical Discourses of Modernity: Twelve Lectures.* Trans. Frederich Lawrence. Cambridge, MA: MIT P, 1992.
Hamilton, A.C. *Northrop Frye: An Anatomy of his Criticism.* Toronto: U of Toronto P, 1990.
Hart, Jonathon. *Northrop Frye and the Theoretical Imagination.* New York and London: Routledge, 1994.
– 'Frye's Anatomizing and Anatomizing Frye.' *Canadian Review of Comparative Literature* 19.1–2 (Mar./June 1992): 119–54.
Hartman, Geoffrey. 'Ghostlier Demarcations.' *Northrop Frye in Modern Criticism.* Ed. Murray Krieger. New York: Columbia UP, 1966. 109–31.
Hassan, Ihab. 'Beyond a Theory of Literature: Intimations of Apocalypse?' *Comparative Literature Studies* 1.4 (1964): 261–71.
– 'Confessions of a Reluctant Critic; or, The Resistance to Literature.' *New Literary History* 24.1 (Winter 1993): 1–16.
Herrnstein Smith, Barbara. *Contingencies of Value: Alternative Perspectives for Critical Theory.* Cambridge, MA: Harvard UP, 1988.
– 'The Unquiet Judge: Activism without Objectivism in Law and Politics.' *Rethinking Objectivity.* Annals of Scholarship. Ed. Allan Megill. 1992.
Hertz, Neil. *The End of the Line: Essays in the Psychoanalysis of the Sublime.* New York: Columbia UP, 1985.
Hipple, W.J. *The Beautiful, the Sublime, and the Picturesque in Eighteenth-Century British Poetic Theory.* Carbondale: Illinois UP, 1957.

Hirsch, E.D. *The Aims of Interpretation*. Chicago: U of Chicago P, 1976.
– 'Literary Evaluation as Knowledge.' *Contemporary Literature* 9 (Summer 1968): 319–31.
Holquist, Michael. 'Introduction.' *Art and Answerability: Early Philosophical Essays by M.M. Bakhtin*. Trans. Vadim Liapunov. Austin: U of Texas P, 1990.
Hughes, Peter. 'Creativity and History in Vico and His Contemporaries.' Tagliacozzo and Verene 155–69.
– 'Vico and Literary History.' *Yale Italian Studies* 1 (Winter 1977): 83–90.
Hutcheon, Linda. *Narcissistic Narrative: The Metafictional Paradox*. New York: Methuen, 1980.
Jameson, Frederic. *The Prison-House of Language: A Critical Account of Structuralism and Russian Formalism*. Princeton: Princeton UP, 1972.
Jaynes, Julian. *The Origin of Consciousness in the Breakdown of the Bicameral Mind*. Boston: Houghton Mifflin, 1976.
Kant, Immanuel. *Critique of Judgment*. 1790. Trans. Werner S. Pluhar. Indianapolis: Hachett, 1987.
Kermode, Frank. 'Northrop Frye.' *Puzzles and Epiphanies: Essays and Reviews, 1958–1961*. London: Routledge and Kegan Paul, 1962.
Krieger, Murray. 'The Mirror as Window in Recent Literary Theory: Contextualism and its Alternatives.' *A Window to Criticism: Shakespeare's Sonnets and Recent Poetics*. Princeton: Princeton UP, 1964. 28–70.
Krieger, Murray, ed. *Northrop Frye in Modern Criticism: Selected Papers from the English Institute*. New York: Columbia UP, 1966.
Kushner, Eva. 'Northrop Frye et la possibilité du dialogue interculturel.' *Recherches Sémiotiques/Semiotic Inquiry* 13.3 (1993): 23–31.
Lee, Alvin A., and Robert D. Denham, eds. *The Legacy of Northrop Frye*. Toronto: U of Toronto P, 1994.
– 'Northrop Frye: Identity not Negation.' *Recherches Sémiotiques/Semiotic Inquiry* 13.3 (1993): 33–46.
Lentricchia, Frank. *After the New Criticism*. Chicago: U of Chicago P, 1980.
Longinus. 'On the Sublime.' *Classical Literary Criticism*. Trans. and intro. T.S. Dorsch. Markham, ON: Penguin, 1965. 97–158.
Lowe, Victor. 'Whitehead's Metaphysical System.' *Process Philosophy and Christian Thought*. Ed. Delwin Brown, Ralph E. James, Jr., and Gene Reeves. New York: Bobbs-Merrill, 1971. 3–20.
Lowth, Robert. *Lectures on the Sacred Poetry of the Hebrews*. 1787. Trans. G. Gregory. New York: Garland, 1971.
Lyotard, Jean-François. *L'Inhumain: Causeries sur le temps*. Paris: Éditions Galilée, 1988.

– *The Postmodern Condition: A Report on Knowledge.* Trans. Geoff Bennington and Brian Massumi. Minneapolis: U of Minnesota P, 1984.

Mali, Joseph. *The Rehabilitation of Myth: Vico's New Science.* New York: Cambridge UP, 1992.

Manuel, Frank. *The Eighteenth-Century Confronts the Gods.* Cambridge: Harvard UP, 1959.

Mellert, Robert B. *What is Process Theology?* New York: Paulist Press, 1975.

Milbank, John. *The Religious Dimension in the Thought of Giambattista Vico, 1668–1744.* Lewiston, ON: Edwin Mellen Press, 1991.

Modica, Giuseppe. 'Umanesimo e corporietà in Vico.' *Giambattista Vico: Poesia, logica, religione.* Brescia: Marceliana, 1986. 352–66.

Monk, Samuel. *The Sublime: A Study of Critical Theories in XVIII-Century England.* Ann Arbor: U of Michigan P, 1960.

Morris, D.B. *The Religious Sublime: Christian Poetry and Critical Tradition in 18th-Century England.* Lexington: UP of Kent, 1972.

Neussel, Frank. 'Metaphor and Cognition: A Review Essay.' *Metaphor, Communication and Cognition.* Ed. Marcel Danesi. Toronto Semiotic Circle, monograph series 2 (1987–8): 87–98.

Nicolson, Marjorie Hope. *Mountain Gloom and Mountain Glory: The Development of the Aesthetic of the Infinite.* Ithaca, NY: Cornell UP, 1959.

O'Hara, Daniel. *The Romance of Interpretation: Visionary Criticism from Pater to de Man.* New York: Columbia UP, 1985.

Pietropaolo, Domenico. *Dante Studies in the Age of Vico.* Ottawa: Dovehouse, 1989.

– 'Frye, Blake, e la boria dei dotti.' *Allegoria: per uno studio materialistico della letteratura* 1.3 (1989): 134–8.

– 'Frye, Vico, and the Grounding of Literature and Criticism.' *Ritratto di Northrop Frye.* Ed. Agostino Lombardo. Roma: Bulzoni, 1990. 87–104.

– 'Northrop Frye.' *I discorsi della critica in America.* Ed. John Picchione. Roma: Bulzoni, 1993. 23–37.

– 'Northrop Frye e la paideia della libertà.' *Belfagor* 4 (1992): 403–18.

Riccomini, Donald R. 'Northrop Frye and Structuralism: Identity and Difference.' *University of Toronto Quarterly* 49 (Fall 1979): 33–47.

Ricoeur, Paul. '*Anatomy of Criticism* or the Order of Paradigms.' *Centre and Labyrinth: Essays in Honour of Northrop Frye.* Ed. Eleanor Cook et al. Toronto: U of Toronto P, 1983. 1–13.

Rothstein, Eric. 'Anatomy and Bionomics of Criticism: Eighteenth-Century Cases.' *Eighteenth-Century Studies* 24.2 (Winter 1990–91): 197–223.

Russo, Luigi, ed. *Da Longino a Longino: I luoghi del Sublime.* Palermo: Aesthetica, 1987.

Said, Edward. *Beginnings: Intention and Method.* New York: Basic Books, 1975.

– 'Vico: Autodidact and Humanist.' *The Centennial Review of Arts and Science* 11 (1967): 336–52.

Saint Girons, Baldine. *Fiat Lux: Une Philosophie du Sublime.* Paris: Quai Voltaire, 1993.

Schaeffer, John D. 'From Wit to Narration: Vico's Theory of Metaphor in its Rhetorical Context.' *New Vico Studies* 2 (1984): 59–73.

– *Sensus Communis: Vico, Rhetoric and the Limits of Relativism.* Durham: Duke UP, 1990.

Sparshott, Francis. 'The Riddle of *Katharsis.*' *Centre and Labyrinth.* Ed. Eleanor Cook et al. Toronto: U of Toronto P, 1983. 14–37.

Steinke, Horst. 'Hintikka and Vico: An Update on Contemporary Logic.' *New Vico Studies* 3 (1985): 147–55.

Tagliacozzo, Giorgio, and Donald Philip Verene, eds. *Giambattista Vico's Science of Humanity.* Baltimore: Johns Hopkins UP, 1976.

Tagliacozzo, Giorgio, and Hayden White, eds. *Giambattista Vico: An International Symposium.* Baltimore: Johns Hopkins UP, 1969.

Vattimo, Gianni. *La fine della modernità.* Milano: Garzanti, 1985.

Verene, Donald Phillip. 'Introduction.' *On Humanistic Education: Six Inaugural Orations, 1699–1707.* Trans. Giorgio A. Pinton and Arthur W. Shippee. Ithaca, NY: Cornell UP, 1993.

– 'The New Art of Narration: Vico and the Muses.' *New Vico Studies* 1 (1983): 21–38.

– *Vico's Science of Imagination.* Ithaca, NY: Cornell UP, 1981.

– 'Vico's Science of Imaginative Universals and the Philosophy of Symbolic Forms.' Tagliacozzo and Verene 295–317.

Vico, Giambattista. *The Autobiography of Giambattista Vico.* Trans. Max Harold Fisch and Thomas Goddard Bergin. Ithaca, NY: Cornell UP, 1944.

– *On the Most Ancient Wisdom of the Italians.* 1710. Trans. and intro. L.M. Palmer. Ithaca, NY: Cornell UP, 1988.

– *The New Science.* 1744. Abridged trans. Thomas Goddard and Max Harold Fisch. Ithaca, NY: Cornell UP, 1970.

– *Opere.* Ed. Fausto Nicolini. Milano: Riccardo Ricciardi, 1953.

– *On the Study Methods of Our Time.* 1709. Trans. Elio Gianturco. New York: Bobbs-Merrill, 1965.

Wellek, René. 'The Poet as Critic, the Critic as Poet, the Poet-Critic.' *Discriminations: Further Concepts of Criticism.* New Haven, CT: Yale UP, 1970. 253–74.

Weinbrot, Howard D. 'Northrop Frye and the Literature of Process Reconsidered.' *Eighteenth-Century Studies* 24.2 (Winter 1990–91): 173–95.

Weiskel, Thomas. *The Romantic Sublime: Studies in the Structure and Psychology of Transcendence.* Baltimore: Johns Hopkins UP, 1975.

White Hayden. *Metahistory: The Historical Imagination in Nineteenth-Century Europe*. Baltimore: Johns Hopkins UP, 1973.

– 'The Structure of Hitorical Narrative.' *Clio* 1 (June 1972): 5–20.

– 'The Tropics of History: The Deep Structure of the New Science.' Tagliacozzo and Verene 65–85.

Whitehead, Alfred North. *Process and Reality: An Essay on Cosmology*. Cambridge: Cambridge UP, 1929.

– *Science and the Modern World*. 1925. New York: The Free Press, 1967.

Wimsatt, Jr, W.K., 'Northrop Frye: Criticism as Myth.' *Northrop Frye in Modern Criticism*. Ed. Murray Krieger. New York: Columbia UP, 1966. 75–107.

Index